knitted dinosaurs

knitted dinosaurs

A collection of prehistoric pals to knit from scratch

Tina Barrett

First published 2011 by
Guild of Master Craftsman Publications Ltd
Castle Place, 166 High Street, Lewes,
East Sussex BN7 1XU

Reprinted 2013, 2019

Text and designs © Tina Barrett, 2011
Copyright in the Work © GMC Publications Ltd,
2011

ISBN 978-1-86108-817-8

A catalogue record for this book is available
from the British Library.

Publisher: Jonathan Bailey
Production: Jim Bulley and Jo Pallett
Managing Editor: Gerrie Purcell
Senior Project Editor: Virginia Brehaut
Copy Editor: Beth Wicks
Managing Art Editor: Gilda Pacitti
Design: Rebecca Mothersole and Rob Janes
Photography: Rebecca Mothersole

Set in Frutiger
Colour origination by GMC Reprographics
Printed and bound in China

Where those prehistoric pals roam

The dinosaurs

Introduction

When I was first approached about working on a book of knitted dinosaurs, by coincidence, my youngest daughter was completely obsessed with the film *Jurassic Park* and anything else with a prehistoric theme. We were surrounded by dino books, a roaring plastic Spinosaurus and even a 'hungry dinosaur' game. Therefore, I felt well qualified (one step away from being an expert palaeontologist in fact) to tackle the challenge of creating some woolly dinosaurs with my own needles and yarn.

It really turned out to be a fun journey where I got to learn even more dino facts along the way. Each character suddenly woke up and came alive the moment I finished modelling its eyes, and it's true to say that by the end, I became quite attached to each and every one. As I lined them all up around my studio, friends would drop by and tell me of a child or grandchild they knew who would love to own one.

If it turns out that you are also someone who knows a dino-mad child (or adult), then this is the ideal book for you. I have kept things simple throughout, using only DK and Chunky-weight yarn. The amounts used per pattern are relatively small so each dinosaur could also work as an ideal stash-busting project.

Even though science can tell us what shape, how big or how many spines each dinosaur had by looking at fossils, no one can definitively tell us what colour they were. This means that the mighty T-Rex might have been hot pink with purple spots and if you decide to knit him that colour then no one can argue with you! So, don't just go with the colours I have used. Try experimenting with yours or your child's favourites. Go wild in your own imagination and by doing that you are bound to create your own individual character. Choose different-coloured eyes to make him as cute or scary as you dare.

Good luck and please, go and have fun with those needles.

Tina Barrett

TRICERATOPS >> 46

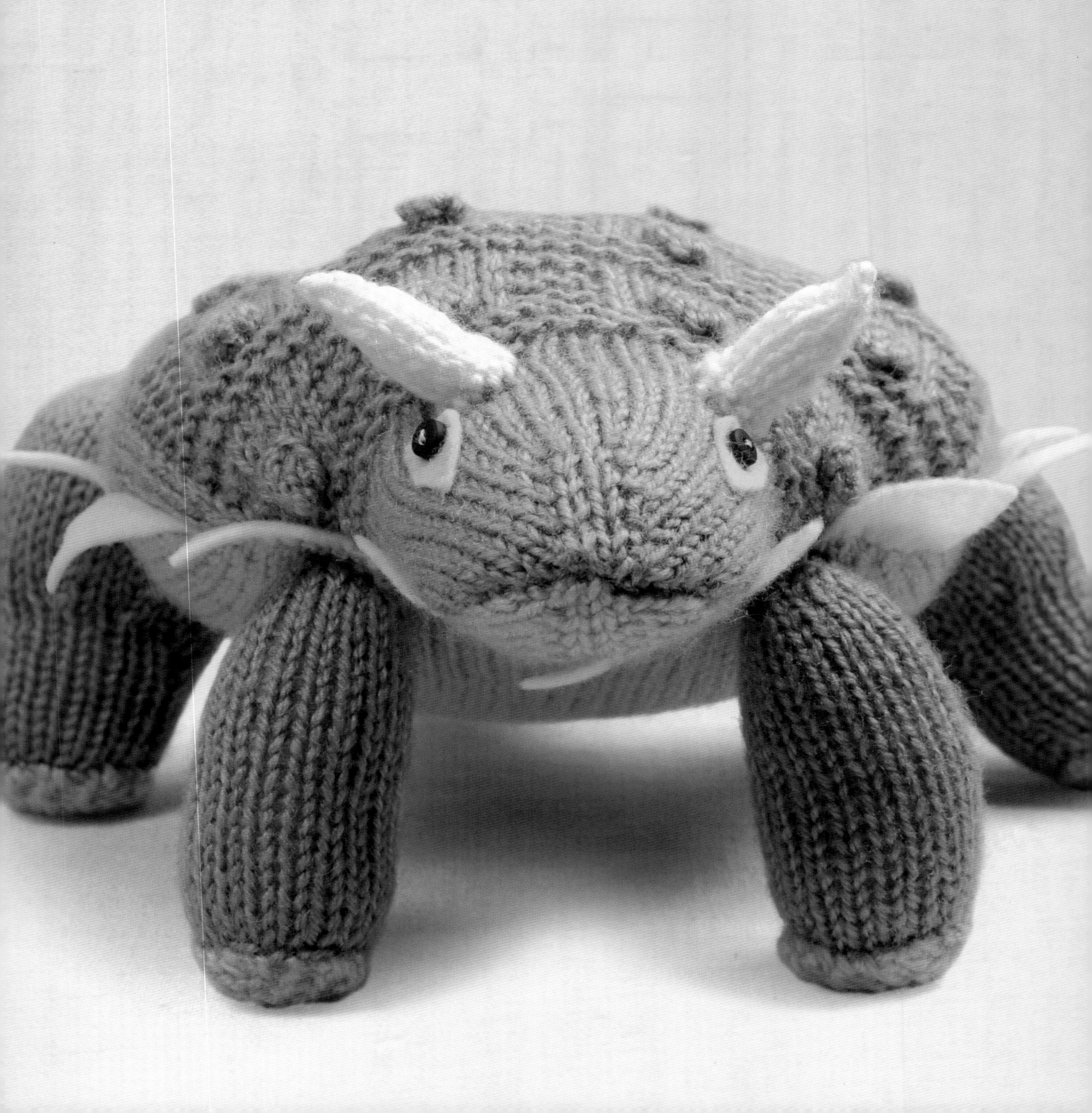

PARASAUROLOPHUS >> 58

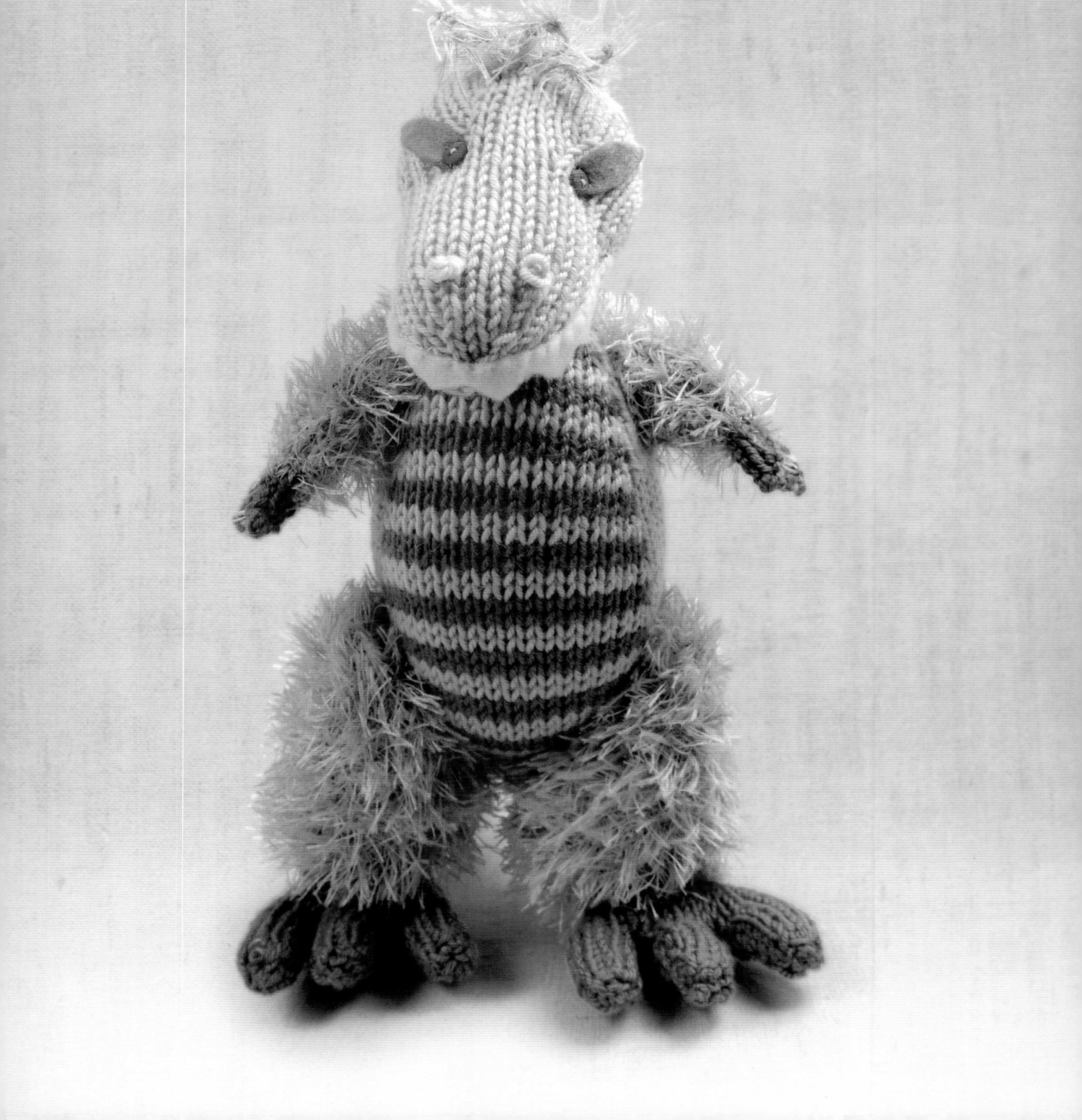

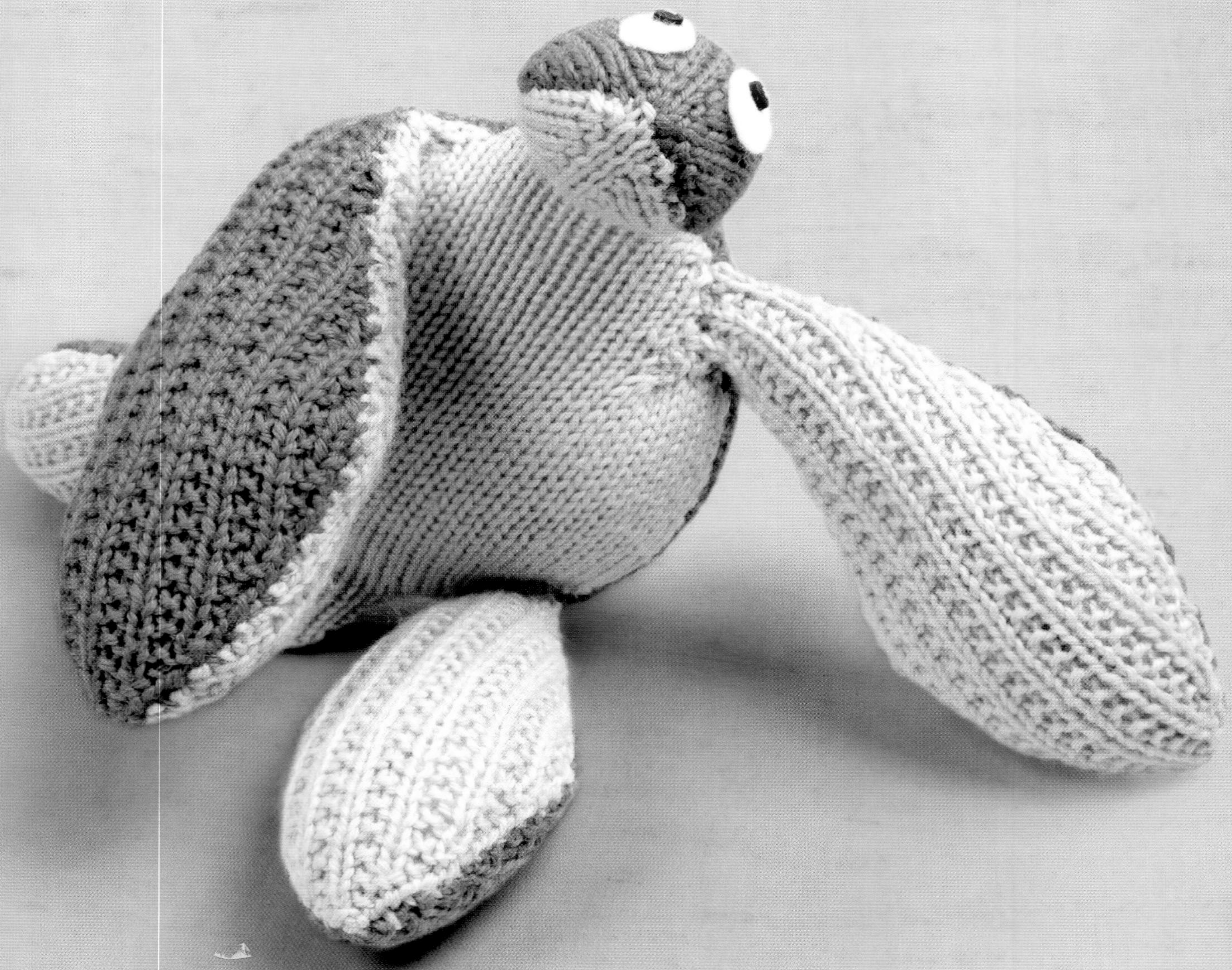

PTERODACTYL >> 100

A T-Rex with a gentle nature

Beady-eyed Quetzalcoatlus

Athletic Velociraptor

Ferocious Spinosaurus

Dippy Diplodocus

The dinosaurs

Diplodocus were long-necked, whip-tailed giants. Their main food was probably conifers, supplemented by gingkos, ferns, club mosses and horsetails. They used their incredibly long necks to poke into forests and across unstable wetland areas to reach foliage and soft-leaved plants.

DIPLODOCUS

Information you'll need

Finished size

Diplodocus measures 31in (78cm)
from nose to tail

Materials

Stylecraft Life Super Chunky 75% acrylic,
25% wool (80m per 100g)
1 x 100g ball in Denim (A)
1 x 100g ball in Cream (B)
1 pair of 8mm (UK0:US11) needles
An old pair of jeans
Yellow thread
Small piece of white felt for eyes
2 small brown buttons (approx. ³⁄₁₆in/5mm)
Fabric glue
Polyester toy stuffing

Tension

10.5 sts x 15 rows to 4in (10cm) over
st st using 8mm needles.
Use larger or smaller needles if necessary
to obtain correct tension.

Don't let Diplodocus stand on your toe. He weighs more than a double-decker bus!

How to make Diplodocus

Stripe pattern

4 rows A

4 rows B

Note: work in stripe pattern throughout unless otherwise stated.

Body: worked from nose to tail (make 1)

Head

Using A, cast on 6 sts.

Row 1: Kfb into each stitch (12 sts).

Row 2 and all alt rows: Purl.

Row 3: (K1, kfb) 6 times (18 sts).

Row 5: (K2, kfb) 6 times (24 sts).

Keeping to stripe patt, work 7 rows in stocking stitch.

Neck

Row 1: (K2, k2tog) 6 times (18 sts).

Row 2: Purl.

Row 3: (K1, k2tog) 6 times (12 sts).

Row 4: Purl.

Keeping to stripe patt, work 20 rows in stocking stitch.

Belly

Inc 1 st at each end of next and every foll row to 36 sts.

Work in stocking stitch for a further 7in (18cm), ending on a purl row.

Tail

Dec 1 st at each end of every row to 12 sts.

Work in stocking stitch for 20 rows.

Dec 1 st at each end of every row to 2 sts.

Next row: K2tog and fasten off.

Back legs (make 2)

Using A, cast on 10 sts.

Row 1: Kfb to end of row (20 sts).

Row 2: Purl.

Row 3: (K3, kfb) 5 times (25 sts).

Row 4: Purl.

Change to B and work 4 rows in st st.

Change to A.

Next row: (K2tog) rep to last st, k1 (13 sts).

Work 3 rows in st st.

Change to B and work 20 rows in st st in stripe pattern.

Cast off.

Front legs (make 2)

Work as for back legs.

Sole template (100%)

Making up

Sew in loose yarn ends. Fold body in half
lengthwise and sew belly seam leaving a
small opening for stuffing. Stuff firmly and
close opening. Fold all four legs in half and
sew rear seam. Stuff firmly through sole
with stuffing. Cut out circles of denim from
the jeans using the sole template above.
Using simple back stitch and yellow thread,
sew a circle in the centre of the denim
sole (refer to photos). Repeat for the other
three. Stitch a sole to the end of each leg,
tucking the edges in as you go. Cut two
back pockets from the jeans and sew to
each side of Diplodocus. Position the legs
onto Diplodocus and sew firmly in place.
Cut two large teardrop shapes of white
felt for eyes and glue in place with fabric
glue. Sew a button on the top of each eye
towards the bottom.

Triceratops were slow, bulky dinosaurs with short, pointed tails, four sturdy legs with hoof-like claws and bony neck frills. One short horn above their parrot-like beaks and two longer horns above their eyes provided protection from predators. When threatened, Triceratops charged towards its enemy like a rhinoceros.

TRICERATOPS

Information you'll need

Finished size

Triceratops measures 18in (46cm) from
nose to tail

Materials

Rico Essentials Merino DK
100% merino (120m per 50g)
2 x 50g balls in Red (05) (A)
1 x 50g ball in Jeans (27) (B)
1x 50g ball in Natural (60) (C)
1 pair of 3mm (UK11:US2–3) needles
1 square of blue felt for spots
Small amount of white felt for eyes
2 small brown buttons (approx. ³⁄₁₆in/5mm)
Fabric glue
Polyester toy stuffing

Tension

26 sts and 36 rows to 4in (10cm)
over st st using 3mm needles.
Use larger or smaller needles
if necessary to obtain correct tension.

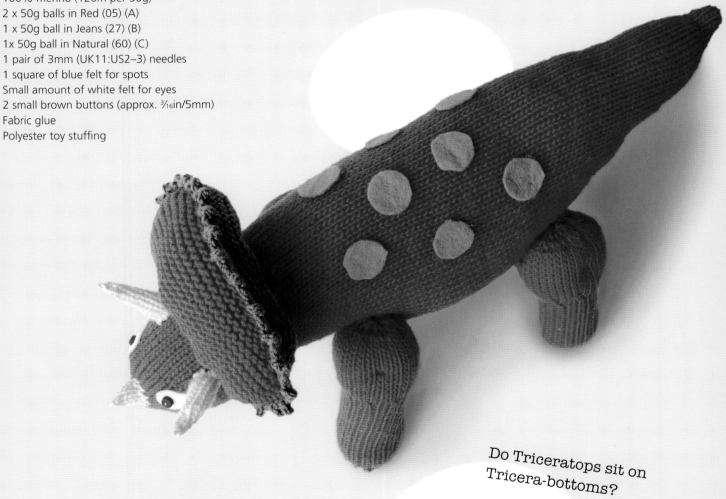

Do Triceratops sit on
Tricera-bottoms?

How to make Triceratops

Body: worked from nose to tail (make 1)

Head

Using A, cast on 6 sts.
Row 1: Kfb into each stitch (12 sts).
Row 2 and every foll alt row: Purl.
Row 3: (K1, kfb) 6 times (18 sts).
Row 5: (K2, kfb) 6 times (24 sts).
Row 7: (K3, kfb) 6 times (30 sts).
Row 9: (K4, kfb) 6 times (36 sts).
Work 6 rows in st st.

Neck

Row 1: (K5, kfb) 6 times (42 sts).
Work 9 rows.
Row 11: (K5, k2tog) 6 times (36 sts).
Work 5 rows.
Row 17: (K5, kfb) 6 times (42 sts).
Row 18: Purl.
Working in st st, inc 1 st at each end of every row to 66 sts.
Work in st st for a further 44 rows, ending on a WS row.

Tail

Dec 1 st at each end of every row to 26 sts, ending on a WS row.
Work 17 rows.
Dec 1 st at each end of every row to 2 sts.
Next row: P2tog and fasten off.

Back legs (make 2)

Using A, cast on 10 sts.
Row 1: Kfb into each st (20 sts).
Row 2 and every foll alt row: Purl.
Row 3: (K1, kfb) 10 times (30 sts). **
Row 5: (K2, kfb) 10 times (40 sts).
Row 6: Purl.
Work 10 rows in st st.
Next row: (K2, k2tog) 10 times (30 sts).
Next row: Purl.
Next row: (K1, k2tog) 10 times (20 sts).
Next row: Purl.
Work 20 rows in st st.
Cast off.

Front legs (make 2)

Using A, cast on 10 sts and work as for back legs to **.
Row 5: Purl.
Work 12 rows in st st.
Next row: (K1, k2tog) 10 times (20 sts).
Next row: Purl.
Work 20 rows in st st.
Cast off.

Soles (make 4)

Using B, cast on 4 sts.
Row 1: Kfb, k2, kfb (6 sts).
Row 2 and every foll alt row: Knit.
Row 3: Kfb, k4, kfb (8 sts).
Row 5: Kfb, k6, kfb (10 sts).
Row 7: K2tog, k6, k2tog (8 sts).
Row 9: K2tog, k4, ktog (6 sts).
Row 11: K2tog, k2, k2tog (4 sts).
Cast off.

Nose horn (make 1)

Using C, cast on 12 sts.
Knit 1 row.
Beg with a P row, working in st st, dec 1 st at each end of the next and every foll row to 2 sts.
Next row: K2tog and fasten off.
Sew the long seam of the horn and stuff lightly with toy stuffing.

LOOK!
This poor creature is looking for an alternative style of neck frill. What are his chances?

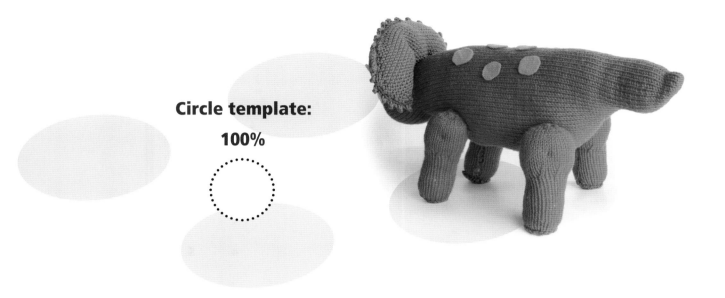

Circle template:

100%

Head horns (make 2)

Using C, cast on 8 sts.

Work 4 rows in st st.

Dec 1 st at each end of next row (6 sts).

Work 3 rows.

Dec 1 st at each end of next row (4 sts).

Work 3 rows.

Next row: (K2tog) twice (2 sts).

Next row: K2tog and fasten off.

Sew the long seam of the horns and stuff lightly with toy stuffing.

Neck frill

worked from top of frill to neck edge (make 1 in A and 1 in B)

Cast on 22 sts.

Working in g st throughout, cont as folls:-

Inc 1 st at each end of every row to 40 sts.

Work straight for 1½in (4cm), ending with a P row.

Next row: (K2tog) 20 times (20 sts).

Cast off.

Picot edge

Take the red piece and using B, pick up and knit 34 sts around the top edge of the neck frill, turn and work picot cast off as folls:

Picot Cast off: Cast off 3 sts, * cast on 2 sts in the stitch on your LH needle, cast off 4 sts, rep from * to last end. Fasten off.

Frill

Place both pieces together and sew around all edges except the lower edge. Stuff lightly and close the neck edge seam.

Making up

Sew in loose yarn ends.

Body

Fold body in half lengthwise and sew belly seam leaving a small opening for stuffing. Stuff firmly and close opening.

Legs

Fold all four legs in half and sew rear seam. Stuff firmly through sole with stuffing. Sew a sole onto the bottom of each leg. Position the legs onto Triceratops and sew firmly in place, making sure they are all even and he can stand up on a flat surface.

Additional features

Sew the neck frill to the base of Triceratops neck. Cut two teardrop shapes of white felt for eyes and glue in place with fabric glue. Sew a button on the top of each eye. Sew the nose horn onto the nose tip. Position each head horn according to the photo and sew firmly in place. Cut eight circles of blue felt, using the template above, and stick them randomly along Triceratops' back using fabric glue.

Ankylosaurus were tank-like dinosaurs, heavily protected by thick oval plates embedded in their leathery skin. They also had two rows of spikes along their bodies, large horns and a club-like tail. Only their underbelly was unplated. Short of being flipped over, the Ankylosaurus was well protected from its predators.

ANKYLOSAURUS

Information you'll need

Finished size
Ankylosaurus measures 14in (36cm) from nose to tail

Materials
Stylecraft Life DK, 75% acrylic, 25% wool (298m per 100g)
1 x 100g ball each in the following shades:
Fern (2311) (A)
White (2300) (B)
Daffodil (2394) (C)
1 pair of 3mm (UK11:US2–3) needles
1 square of white felt for spikes
Fabric glue
2 small brown buttons (approx. ³⁄₁₆in/5mm)
Polyester toy filling

Tension
26 sts and 36 rows to 4in (10cm) over st st using 3mm needles.
Use larger or smaller needles if necessary to obtain correct tension.

DID YOU KNOW?
Ankylosaurus ate huge amounts of plants and would have produced large amounts of gas!

How to make Ankylosaurus

Underbelly: worked nose to tail (make 1)

Using C, cast on 3 sts.
Row 1: Kfb, k1, kfb (5 sts).
Row 2 and every foll alt rows: Purl.
Row 3: K1, kfb, k1, kfb, k1 (7 sts).
Row 5: K2, kfb, k1, kfb, k2 (9 sts).
Row 7: K3, kfb, k1, kfb, k3 (11 sts).
Row 9: K4, kfb, k1, kfb, k4 (13 sts).
Row 11: K5, kfb, k1, kfb, k5 (15 sts).
Row 13: K2tog, k11, k2tog (13 sts).
Row 15: K2tog, k9, k2tog (11 sts).
Work 9 rows straight in st st.
Inc each end of every row to 33 sts then increase on every foll alt row to 41 sts.
Work evenly in stocking stitch until underbelly meas 7½in (19cm) from cast-on edge, ending with RS facing for next row.
Dec 1 st at each end of every row to 13 sts. Work 6 rows.
Dec 1 st at each end of next and every foll alt row to 5 sts.
Work 7 rows, ending with RS facing for next row.
Next row: Kfb into each st (10 sts).
Work 3 rows.
Next row: K2tog to end of row (5 sts).
Next row: Purl.
Next row: K1, (k2tog) twice (3 sts).
Next row: P3tog and fasten off.

Upper body: worked from nose to tail (make 1)

Using A, cast on 3 sts.
Row 1: Kfb, k1, kfb (5 sts).
Row 2 and all alt rows: Purl.
Row 3: (Kfb) twice, k1, (kfb) twice (9 sts).
Row 5: Kfb, k2, kfb, k1, kfb, k2, kfb (13 sts).
Row 7: Kfb, k4, kfb, k1, kfb, k4, kfb (17 sts).
Row 9: Kfb, k6, kfb, k1, kfb, k6, kfb (21 sts).
Row 11: Kfb, k8, kfb, k1, kfb, k8, kfb (25 sts).
Row 12: Purl.
Dec 1 st at each end of next and foll alt rows to 21 sts.
Work 9 rows, ending with RS facing for next row.

Armour plate pattern

Work 4 rows in g st, inc 1 st at each end of every row (29 sts).
Row 1: Kfb, knit, kfb (31 sts).
Row 2: Kfb, purl, kfb (33 sts).
Row 3: Kfb, k3, (MB, k7) 3 times, MB, k3, kfb (35 sts).
Row 4: Kfb, k2, (p5, k3) 3 times, p5, k2, kfb (37 sts).
Row 5: Kfb, k to last st, kfb (39 sts).
Row 6: Kfb, p1, k3, (p5, k3) 4 times, p1, kfb (41 sts).
Row 7: Kfb, k to last st, kfb (43 sts).
Rows 8–11: Knit.
Row 12: P4, k3, (p5, k3) 4 times, p4.
Row 13: K9, (MB, k7) 3 times, MB, k9.
Row 14: As row 12.
Row 15: Knit.
Row 16: As row 12.
Rows 17–20: Knit.
Rep rows 11–20 until upper meas 7½in (19cm) from cast-on edge, ending with RS facing for next row.
Cont in patt and AT SAME TIME, dec 1 st at each end of every row to 17 sts.
Work 6 rows.
Dec 1 st at each end of next and every alt rows to 9 sts.
Work 5 rows.

Tail

Row 1: Kfb to end of row (18 sts).

Work 3 rows in g st.

Row 5: K2tog across row (9 sts).

Row 6: Purl.

Row 7: K1, (k2tog) across row (5 sts).

Row 8: Purl.

Row 9: K1, (k2tog) twice (3 sts).

Row 10: P3tog and fasten off.

Back legs (make 2)

Using A, cast on 10 sts.

Row 1: Kfb into each st (20 sts).

Row 2 and every foll alt row: Purl.

Row 3: (K1, kfb) 10 times (30 sts).

Row 5: (K2, kfb) 10 times (40 sts).

Row 6: Purl.

Work 10 rows in stocking stitch.

Next row: (K2, k2tog) 10 times (30 sts).

Next row: Purl.

Next row: (K1, k2tog) 10 times (20 sts).

Next row: Purl.

Work 10 rows in st st.

Cast off.

Front legs (make 2)

Using A, cast on 10 sts.

Row 1: Kfb into each st (20 sts).

Work 20 rows in st st.

Cast off.

Soles (make 4)

Using C, cast on 4 sts.

Row 1: Kfb, k2, kfb (6 sts).

Row 2 and every foll alt row: Knit.

Row 3: Kfb, k4, kfb (8 sts).

Row 5: Kfb, k6, kfb (10 sts).

Row 7: K2tog, k6, k2tog (8 sts).

Row 9: K2tog, k4, k2tog (6 sts).

Row 11: K2tog, k2, k2tog (4 sts).

Cast off.

Tail clubs (make 3)

Using C, cast on 6 sts. Working in g st throughout, work as folls;

Row 1: Kfb into every st (12 sts).

Row 2 and every foll alt row: Knit.

Row 3: (K1, kfb) 6 times (18 sts).

Row 5: (K2, kfb) 6 times (24 sts).

Work 1 row.

Change to A.

Row 7: (K2, k2tog) 6 times (18 sts).

Row 9: (K1, k2tog) 6 times (12 sts).

Row 11: (K2tog) 6 times (6 sts).

Break yarn leaving a long tail, thread through rem sts, stuff the club firmly with toy filling and pull the thread tight. Fasten off.

Horns (make 2)

Using B, cast on 8 sts.

Work 4 rows in stocking stitch.

Dec each end of next and every foll alt row to 2 sts.

Next row: Purl.

Next row: K2tog and fasten off.

Making up

Cut the side spikes in white felt using the templates below. Sew the upper to the lower half, sandwiching the spikes between the two parts (refer to photo). Leave a small opening for stuffing. Stuff the body firmly and close the opening. Sew another spike to the underside of the chin. Sew the three clubs to the tail tip. Sew the rear seam of each leg. Stuff firmly with toy filling and sew a sole over the end of each leg. Position the legs and sew firmly to the sides of your dinosaur. Sew the horns on top of the head. Cut two teardrop-shaped pieces of white felt for eyes. Stick in place with fabric glue and sew a small button on top of each.

Spikes template: 100%

Cut 6 big spikes and 5 small spikes.

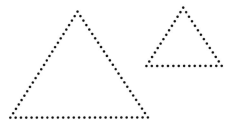

Stegosaurus means 'plated lizard', which refers to the large bony plates that ran along the back and tail in two rows. They also had spikes at the end of their flexible tails. Stegosauruses were similar in size to a bus, with small heads about the same size as a horse!

STEGOSAURUS

Information you'll need

Finished size
Stegosaurus measures 18in (46cm)
from nose to tail

Materials
Rico Merino Essentials DK 100% merino
(120m per 50g)
2 x 50g balls each in the following shades:
Mulberry (19) (A)
Sun (66) (B)
1 pair of 3mm (UK11:US2–3) needles
Small piece of yellow felt for eyes
2 small brown buttons (approx. ³/₁₆in/5mm)
Polyester toy filling

Tension
26 sts and 36 rows over
4in (10cm) to st st using
3mm needles.
Use larger or smaller
needles if necessary to
obtain correct tension.

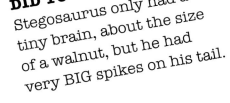

DID YOU KNOW?
Stegosaurus only had a
tiny brain, about the size
of a walnut, but he had
very BIG spikes on his tail.

How to make Stegosaurus

Body: worked from nose to tail (make 1)

Head

Using A, cast on 6 sts.

Row 1: Kfb into each stitch (12 sts).
Row 2 and every foll alt row: Purl.
Row 3: (K1, kfb) 6 times (18 sts).
Row 5: (K2, kfb) 6 times (24 sts).
Row 7: (K3, kfb) 6 times (30 sts).
Row 9: (K4, kfb) 6 times (36 sts).
Work 6 rows in st st.

Neck

Row 1: (K4, k2tog) 6 times (30 sts).
Row 2 and every foll alt row: Purl.
Row 3: (K3, k2tog) 6 times (24 sts).
Row 5: (K2, k2tog) 6 times (18 sts).
Row 6: Purl.
Work 14 rows in st st.

Body

Row 1: (K2, kfb) 6 times (24 sts).
Row 2 and every foll alt row: Purl.
Row 3: (K3, kfb) 6 times (30 sts).

Row 5: (K4, kfb) 6 times (36 sts).
Row 7: (K5, kfb) 6 times (42 sts).
Row 8: Purl.
Working in st st, inc 1 st at each end of every row to 66 sts.
Work in st st for a further 44 rows, ending on a WS row.
Dec 1 st at each end of every row to 26 sts, ending on a WS row.

Tail

Work in st st for 22 rows.
Dec 1 st at each end of next and every foll alt row to 14 sts. Purl 1 row.
Dec 1 st at each end of every row to 2 sts.
Next row: K2tog and fasten off.

Back legs (make 2)

Using A, cast on 10 sts.
Row 1: Kfb into every st (20 sts).
Row 2 and every foll alt row: Purl.
Row 3: (K1, kfb) 10 times (30 sts) **.
Row 5: (K2, kfb) 10 times (40 sts).
Row 6: Purl.
Work 10 rows in st st.
Next row: (K2, k2tog) 10 times (30 sts).
Next row: Purl.
Next row: (K1, k2tog) 10 times (20 sts).
Next row: Purl.
Work 20 rows in st st.
Cast off.

Front legs (make 2)

Using A, cast on 10 sts and work as for back legs to **.
Row 4: Purl.
Work 12 rows in st st.
Next row: (K1, k2tog) 10 times (20 sts).
Next row: Purl.
Work 20 rows in st st.
Cast off.

Soles (make 4)

Using B, cast on 4 sts.
Row 1: Kfb, k2, kfb (6 sts).
Row 2 and every foll alt row: Knit.
Row 3: Kfb, k4, kfb (8 sts).
Row 5: Kfb, k6, kfb (10 sts).
Row 7: K2tog, k6, k2tog (8 sts).
Row 9: K2tog, k4, k2tog (6 sts).
Row 11: K2tog, k2, k2tog (4 sts).
Cast off.

Large armour plates (make 12)

Using B, cast on 6 sts.
Using g st throughout, inc 1 st at each end of next and every foll alt row to 16 sts.
Work 6 rows in g st.
Dec 1 st at each end of next and every foll alt rows until 2 sts.
Next row: K2tog and fasten off.

Small armour plates (make 12)

Using B cast on 6 sts.
Knit 1 row.
Row 2: Sl1, k1, psso, k2, ssk (4 sts).
Row 3: Knit.
Row 4: Sl1, k1, psso, ssk (2 sts).
Row 5: Sl1, k1, psso and fasten off.

Don't leave Steggie out in the rain or he'll Stegosaur-rust!

Tail spikes (make 2)
Using B, cast on 16 sts.
Row 1: Kfb, k14, kfb (18 sts).
Row 2: Kfb, k16, kfb (20 sts).
Row 3: K2tog, k14, k2tog (18 sts).
Row 4: K2tog, k12, k2tog (16 sts).
Cast off.

Making up
Sew in loose yarn ends.

Body
Fold body in half lengthwise and sew belly seam leaving a small opening for stuffing. Stuff firmly and close opening.

Legs
Fold all four legs in half and sew rear seam. Stuff firmly though sole with stuffing. Sew a sole onto the bottom of each leg. Position the legs onto the stegosaurus and sew firmly in place, making sure they are all even and he can stand up on a flat surface.

Armoured plates and spikes
Sew six pairs of the large armour plates together leaving a hole at the bottom for stuffing. Stuff fairly firmly and close the opening. Arrange two rows of armour plating down his back (refer to photo) and sew the plates firmly in place. Fold the tail spikes in half lengthwise and sew the seam. They will curl upwards. Place them onto the tail tip and secure in the centre.

Facial features
Cut two teardrop shapes of yellow felt for eyes and glue in place with fabric glue. Sew a button on the top of each eye.

Parasaurolophus were duck-billed dinosaurs with pebbly-textured skin, toothless horny beaks and pointed tails. Their extremely long, hollow crests were used to produce low, foghorn-like sounds in courtship displays. Their sight and hearing were keen, but they had no natural defences.

PARASAUROLOPHUS

Information you'll need

Finished size
Parasaurolophus measures 16in (41cm)
from nose to tail

Materials
Artesano Superwash Merino DK 100%
merino (112m per 50g)
1 x 50g ball each in shades:
Lime green (6315) (A)
Sand yellow (7254) (B)
Cream (SFN10) (C)
Cocoa (SFN33) (D)
1 pair of 3mm (UK11:US2–3) needles
2 wood buttons (approx. $^9/_{16}$in/15mm)
Small piece of white felt for eyes
Fabric glue
2 small brown buttons (approx. $^3/_{16}$in/5mm)

Tension
26 sts and 30 rows over 4in (10cm)
over st st using 3mm needles.
Use larger or smaller needles
if necessary to obtain correct tension.

How to make Parasaurolophus

Stripe pattern

4 rows A/4 rows B/4 rows C/4 rows D

Tail (make 1)

Using A, cast on 32 sts.
Beg with a K row, working in st st and stripe rep throughout. Cont as folls:- work 12 rows. Dec 1 st at each end of next and every foll 3rd row to 16 sts. Dec 1 st at each end of next and every foll row to 2 sts.
Next row: K2tog and fasten off.

Body (make 1)

Head

Using A, cast on 3 sts. Keeping to stripe pattern work as folls:
Row 1: Kfb, k1, kfb (5 sts).
Row 2 and every foll alt row: Purl.
Row 3: Kfb, kfb, k1, kfb, kfb (9 sts).
Row 5: Kfb, k2, kfb, k1, kfb, k2, kfb (13 sts).
Row 7: Kfb, k4, kfb, k1, kfb, k4, kfb (17 sts).
Row 9: Kfb, k6, kfb, k1, kfb, k6, kfb (21 sts).
Row 11: Kfb, k8, kfb, k1, kfb, k8, kfb (25 sts).
Row 13: Kfb, k10, kfb, k1, kfb, k10, kfb (29 sts).
Row 15: Kfb, k12, kfb, k1, kfb, k12, kfb (33 sts).
Row 17: Kfb, k14, kfb, k1, kfb, k14, kfb (37 sts).
Row 19: K16, ssk, k1, k2tog, k16 (35 sts).
Row 20: P15, p2tog, p1, p2togtbl, p15 (33 sts).
Row 21: K14, ssk, k1, k2tog, k14 (31 sts).
Row 22: P13, p2tog, p1, p2togtbl, p13 (29 sts). Rep these 2 decrease rows as set, working one less stitch before the decreases until 21 sts rem.

Neck

Keeping to stripe pattern work as folls:
Row 1: Kfb, k7, ssk, k1, k2tog, k7, kfb (21 sts).
Row 2: Purl. Rep these last 2 rows 3 times more.
Row 9: Kfb, k8, kfb, k1, kfb, k8, kfb (25 sts).
Row 10 and every foll alt row: Purl.
Row 11: Kfb, k10, kfb, k1, kfb, k10, kfb (29 sts).
Row 13: Kfb, k12, kfb, k1, kfb, k12, kfb (33 sts).
Row 15: Kfb, k14, kfb, k1, kfb, k14, kfb (37 sts).
Row 16: Purl.

Belly

Keeping to stripe patt, inc 1 st at each end of next and every foll row to 53 sts.
Row 1: Kfb, k23, ssk, k1, k2tog, k23, kfb (53 sts).
Row 2: Purl. Rep these last 2 rows 11 times more. Dec 1 st at each end of next and every foll alt rows to 45 sts.
Purl 1 row.
Next row: Ssk, k18, ssk, k1, k2tog, k18, k2tog (41 sts).
Row 2: P2tog, p16, p2tog, p1, p2togtbl p16, p2togtbl (37 sts).
Row 3: Ssk, k14, ssk, k1, k2tog, k14, k2tog (33 sts).
Row 4: P2tog, p12, p2tog, p1, p2togtbl p12, p2togtbl (29 sts). Rep these 2 decrease rows as set, working one less stitch before the decreases until 3 sts rem.
Next row: K3tog and fasten off.

Back legs: worked from foot to top of leg (make 2)

Using A, cast on 30 sts. Work 4 rows in st st.

Row 5: K13, ssk, k2tog, k13 (28 sts).
Row 6: P12, p2tog, p2togtbl, p12 (26 sts).
Row 7: K11, ssk, k2tog, k11 (24 sts).
Row 8: P10, p2tog, p2togtbl, p10 (22 sts).
Row 9: K9, ssk, k2tog, k9 (20 sts).
Row 10: Purl. Change to B and cont in stripe patt as folls:- Work 12 rows.

Top of leg
Row 1: (K1, kfb) 10 times (30 sts).
Row 2: Purl.
Row 3: (K2, kfb) 10 times (40 sts).
Row 4: Purl. Work 10 rows.
Next row: (K2, k2tog) 10 times (30 sts).
Next row: Purl.
Next row: (K1, k2tog) 10 times (20 sts).
Next row: Purl.
Next row: (K2tog) 10 times (10 sts). Break yarn leaving a long tail, thread through rem stitches, pull tight and fasten off.

Sole (make 2)

Using B, cast on 4 sts. Working in g st throughout, inc 1 st at each end of every row to 12 sts. Work 6 rows. Dec 1 st at each end of every row to 4 sts. Cast off.

Front legs (make 2)

Using A, cast on 4 sts. Beg stripe patt and work as folls;
Row 1: Kfb into each st (8 sts).
Row 2 and every foll alt row: Purl.
Row 3: (K1, kfb) 4 times (12 sts).
Row 5: (K2, kfb) 4 times (16 sts).
Work 7 rows.
Next row: (K2, k2tog) 4 times (12 sts).
Work 3 rows.
Next row: (K1, k2tog) 4 times (8 sts).
Work 5 rows.

Claws

Row 1: K4, turn and work on these sts only.
Row 2: Purl.
Row 3: (K2tog) twice (2 sts).
Row 4: Purl.
Row 5: K2tog and fasten off. With RS facing, rejoin yarn to last 4 sts. Work rows 1–5 once more.

Head horn (make 1)

Using D cast on 4 sts. Work 12 rows in g st. Inc 1 st at each end of next and every foll row to 14 sts. Work 3 rows. Dec 1 st at each end of next and foll alt rows to 2 sts.
Next row: P2tog and fasten off.

Making up
Body and tail

Fold body in half lengthwise and sew seam leaving a small opening for stuffing. Stuff firmly and close opening. Sew rear seam and stuff tail firmly. Slide the tail over the small bottom end of the body, match the stripes and sew the tail onto the body.

Legs

Sew rear seam and stuff firmly through the sole. Sew the sole onto the bottom of the leg. Repeat for second leg. Position legs onto the body. Make sure the legs and tail form a balanced triangle shape so your parasaurolophus will stand up unaided. Sew the legs on firmly. Sew a wooden button onto each leg top. Fold the front legs in half lengthwise and sew up leaving the claw end open. Stuff each leg firmly and sew across the end, leaving the claws free.

Head horn

Fold the v-shaped part of the head horn in half lengthwise and sew this seam. Do not include the cast-on rows as these will fit flat to your parasaurolophus' head. Stuff the horn, shaping it into a backward curve. Fit to the head using the photo as reference and sew in place.

Facial features

Finally, cut two teardrop shapes from white felt and stick in place with fabric glue. Sew a small button on top of each.

The tyrant lizard king was one of the biggest flesh-eating predators of all time. These fierce carnivores had huge heads, 60 thick, bone-crunching teeth and well-developed jaw muscles. They walked on two powerful legs each with a bird-like foot and three large toes, all equipped with menacing claws.

TYRANNOSAURUS REX

Information you'll need

Finished size
T-Rex measures 18in (46cm) from
nose to tail

Materials
Stylecraft Life DK 75% acrylic, 25% wool
(298m per 100g)
1 x 100g ball each in shades:
Olive (2302) (A)
Daffodil (2394) (B)
Claret (2310) (C)
1 pair of 3mm (UK11:US2–3) needles
Yellow and white felt for eyes and teeth

Needle and white sewing thread
2 small red buttons (approx. $\frac{3}{16}$in/5mm)
Fabric glue
Polyester toy stuffing

Tension
26 sts x 36 rows over 4in (10cm) using
3mm needles and stocking stitch.

DID YOU KNOW?
T-Rex was a massive
40ft (12m) long and
15–20ft (4.5–6m) tall.

How to make T-Rex

Body: worked tail to head (make 1)

Using A, cast on 3 sts.
Purl 1 row.
Beg with a K row and working in st st throughout cont as folls:
Inc 1 st at each end of next and every foll alt rows to 17 sts.
Inc 1 st each end of next and every foll 4th row to 33 sts.
Work 13 rows in st st.

Belly

Row 1: Kfb, k14, kfb, k1, kfb, k14, kfb (37 sts).
Row 2: Pfb, p17, k1, p17, pfb (39 sts).
Row 3: Kfb, k17, kfb, k1, kfb, k17, kfb (43 sts).
Row 4: Pfb, p20, k1, p20, pfb (45 sts).
Row 5: Kfb, k20, kfb, k1, kfb, k20, kfb (49 sts).
Row 6: Pfb, p23, k1, p23, pfb (51 sts).
Row 7: Kfb, k23, kfb, k1, kfb, k23, kfb (55 sts).
Row 8: Purl.
Work 8 rows in st st.
Dec 1 st at each end of next and foll 4th row (51 sts).
Work 1 row.
Dec 1 st at each end of next and every foll alt row to 37 sts.
Purl 1 row.

Neck

Row 1: Ssk, k14, ssk, k1, k2tog, k14, k2tog (33 sts).
Row 2: P16, k1, p16.

Row 3: Ssk, k12, ssk, k1, k2tog, k12, k2tog (29 sts).
Row 4: P14, k1, p14.
Row 5: Ssk, k10, ssk, k1, k2tog, k10, k2tog (25 sts).
Row 6: P12, k1, p12.
Row 7: Ssk, k8, ssk, k1, k2tog, k8, k2tog (21 sts).
Row 8: Purl.
Work 4 rows in st st.

Head

Row 1: K9, kfb, k1, kfb, k9 (23 sts).
Row 2: P10, pfb, k1, pfb, p10 (25 sts).
Row 3: K11, kfb, k1, kfb, k11 (27 sts).
Row 4: P12, pfb, k1, pfb, p12 (29 sts).
Row 5: K13, kfb, k1, kfb, k13 (31 sts).
Row 6: P14, pfb, k1, pfb, p14 (33 sts)
Work 6 rows in st st.
Row 13: K14, ssk, k1, k2tog, k14 (31 sts).
Row 14: P13, p2tog, k1, p2togtbl, p13 (29 sts).
Row 15: K12, ssk, k1, k2tog, k12 (27 sts).
Row 16: Purl.
Row 17: Knit.
Row 18: P2tog, P to end of row (26 sts).

Divide for jaws

Row 1: K20, turn, leave rem 6 sts on a holder.

Row 2: P13, turn, leave rem 7 sts on holder.
Working on these 13 sts only, work 6 rows in st st.
Dec 1 st at each end of next and every foll 4th row to 9 sts.
Purl 1 row.
Dec 1 st at each end of next and every foll alt rows until 3 sts rem.
Purl 1 row.
Next row: Sl1, k2tog, psso and fasten off.
For lower jaw, slide both sets of stitches from the stitch holders onto one needle. Make sure they line up without twisting and the RS is facing you for the next row. You want a row of 13 sts which lay parallel below the top jaw.
Work 6 rows in st st.
Dec 1 st at each end of next and every foll 4th row to 9 sts.
Purl 1 row.
Dec 1 st at each end of next and every foll alt rows until 3 sts rem.
Purl 1 row.
Next row: Sl1, k2tog, psso and fasten off.

Mouth gusset (make 1 in C)

Cast on 3 sts.

Beg with a K row and working in st st throughout, cont as folls:

Inc 1 st at each end of next and every foll alt row to 9 sts.

Work 1 row.

Inc 1 st at each end of next and every foll 4th row to 13 sts.

Work 15 rows in st st.

Dec 1 st at each end of next and every foll 4th row to 9 sts.

Work 1 row.

Dec 1 st at each end of next and every foll alt rows to 3 sts.

Purl 1 row.

Next row: Sl1, k2tog, psso and fasten off.

Back legs: worked from foot to top of leg (make 2)

Cast on 30 sts.

Beg with a K row, work 4 rows in stocking stitch.

Row 5: K13, ssk, k2tog, k13 (28 sts).
Row 6: P12, p2tog, p2togtbl, p12 (26 sts).
Row 7: K11, ssk, k2tog, k11 (24 sts).
Row 8: P10, p2tog, p2togtbl, p10 (22 sts).
Row 9: K9, ssk, k2tog, k9 (20 sts).
Row 10: Purl.
Work 12 rows in st st.

Top of leg

Row 1: (K1, kfb) 10 times (30 sts).
Row 2: Purl.
Row 3: (K2, kfb) 10 times (40 sts).
Row 4: Purl.
Work 10 rows in st st.
Next row: (K2, k2tog) 10 times (30 sts).
Next row: Purl.
Next row: (K1, k2tog) 10 times (20 sts).
Next row: Purl.
Next row: (K2tog) 10 times (10 sts).
Break yarn leaving a long tail, thread through rem stitches, pull tight and fasten off.

Sole (make 2)

Using B, cast on 4 sts.

Working in g st throughout cont as folls:

Inc 1 st at each end of every row to 12 sts.

Work 6 rows.

Dec 1 st at each end of every row to 4 sts.

Cast off.

Front legs (make 2)

Using A, cast on 4 sts.

Row 1: Kfb into each st (8 sts).

Row 2 and every foll alt row: Purl.

Row 3: (K1, kfb) 4 times (12 sts).

Row 5: (K2, kfb) 4 times (16 sts).

Work 7 rows in st st.

Next row: (K2, k2tog) 4 times (12 sts).

Work 3 rows in st st.

Next row: (K1, k2tog) 4 times (8 sts).

Work 5 rows in st st.

Change to B and work 2 rows in st st.

Claws

Row 1: K4, turn and work on these sts only.

Row 2: Knit.

Row 3: (K2tog) twice (2 sts).

Row 4: Knit.

Row 5: K2tog and fasten off.

With RS facing, rejoin yarn to last 4 sts. Work rows 1–5 once more.

Spine (make 1)

Using A, cast on 60 sts.

Knit 1 row.

Work Picot cast off as folls:

Picot cast off

Cast off 3 sts, (cast on 2 sts in the stitch on your LH needle, cast off 4 sts) rep brackets to last stitch. Fasten off.

Making up

Darn in loose yarn ends.

Head and body

Sew up belly seam on body and stuff through mouth firmly, leaving the head unstuffed for the moment. Using the purl side of the mouth gusset as the RS, pin the gusset inside the jaws and stitch around each edge leaving a small opening for stuffing. Finish stuffing the head and body and close opening.

Legs

Sew rear seam and stuff firmly through the sole. Sew the sole onto the bottom of the leg. Repeat for second leg. Position legs onto the body. Make sure the legs and tail form a balanced triangle shape so your T-Rex will stand up unaided. Sew the legs on firmly using the thread jointing method (see Finishing Touches page 116). Fold the front legs in half lengthwise and sew up leaving the claw end open. Stuff each leg firmly and sew across the end, leaving the claws free.

Spine

Pin the spine in place from tip of T-Rex's tail to the bottom of his neck. Stitch in place with small slip stitches.

Spots

Using the template below, cut 10 spots in yellow felt. Position them randomly along T-Rex's back and use the fabric glue to stick in place.

Facial features

Cut two teardrop shapes from yellow felt for the eyes. Stick them into place with fabric glue. Sew a small button on top of each. Using A, sew two French knots (see Finishing Touches page 118) for nostrils on top of T-Rex's top jaw (refer to photo).

Teeth

Cut a strip of white felt approx ½in (1cm) wide. Make sure it is long enough to wrap around the top edge of the jaws. Draw a zig-zag line through the centre of the strip with a pencil or soluble marker and cut this line. You should have two zig-zag strips, each with a straight edge. Dab the straight edges with fabric glue. Stick in place along top and bottom edges of jaw (refer to picture for placement). Use the sewing thread and needle to stitch firmly in place along the straight edge.

Spot template: 100%

These huge meat-eating dinosaurs were the largest and most fearsome predators to have ever lived. They walked on powerful hind legs with massive tails, S-shaped necks, and three-fingered hands with sharp eagle-like claws. Their large, impressive jaws were filled with sharp, serrated teeth 2–4in (5–10cm) long, which they used to devour large plant-eating dinosaurs.

ALLOSAURUS

Information you'll need

Finished size
Allosaurus measures 9½in (24cm) in height

Materials
King Cole Bamboo Cotton, 50% bamboo & 50% cotton (220m per 100g)
1 x 100g ball each in shades:
Green (533) (A)
Fuchsia (536) (B)
1 pair of 3mm (UK11:US2–3) needles
White felt for eyes and teeth
Fabric glue
2 small green buttons (approx. ³⁄₁₆in/5mm)
Sewing thread and needles
Polyester toy stuffing

Tension
26 sts x 36 rows over 4in (10cm) using 3mm needles and stocking stitch

DID YOU KNOW?
The name Allosaurus comes from the Greek *allos*, meaning 'strange' or 'different'.

Allosaurus has pondered this question many times. What is it to be different?

How to make Allosaurus

Body back (make 1 in A)
Cast on 6 sts.
Row 1: Kfb into each st (12 sts).
Row 2 and every foll alt row: Purl.
Row 3: (K1, kfb) 6 times (18 sts).
Row 5: (K2, kfb) 6 times (24 sts).
Row 7: (K3, kfb) 6 times (30 sts).
Row 9: (K4, kfb) 6 times (36 sts).
Row 11: (K5, kfb) 6 times (42 sts).
Row 12: Purl.
Work 20 rows in st st.
Row 33: (K5, k2tog) 6 times (36 sts).
Work 3 rows.
Row 37: (K4, k2tog) 6 times (30 sts).
Work 3 rows.
Row 41: (K3, k2tog) 6 times (24 sts).
Work 3 rows.
Row 45: (K2, k2tog) 6 times (18 sts).
Row 46: Purl.
Row 47: (K1, k2tog) 6 times (12 sts).

Row 48: Purl.
Row 49: k2tog across row (6 sts).
Row 50: Purl.
Cast off.

Body front (make 1 in B)
Cast on 4 sts.
Working in g st throughout cont as folls:-
Row 1: Kfb into each st (8 sts).
Inc 1 st at each end of next and every foll alt row to 20 sts.
Work in st st for 11 rows, ending with RS facing for next row.
Dec 1 st at each end of next and every foll 4th row to 8 sts.
Next row: K2tog across row (4 sts).
Cast off.

Tail (make 1 using A)
Cast on 32 sts.
Beg with a K row, work 12 rows in st st.
Dec 1 st at each end of next and every foll

4th row to 16 sts.
Work 1 row.
Dec 1 st at each end of next and every foll alt row to 2 sts.
Next row: K2tog and fasten off.

Head (make 1 using A)
Cast on 6 sts.
Row 1: Kfb into each st (12 sts).
Row 2 and every foll alt row: Purl.
Row 3: (K1, kfb) 6 times (18 sts).
Row 5: (K2, kfb) 6 times (24 sts).
Row 7: (K3, kfb) 6 times (30 sts).
Row 9: (K4, kfb) 6 times (36 sts).
Row 11: (K5, kfb) 6 times (42 sts).
Row 13: (K6, kfb) 6 times (48 sts).
Work 11 rows in st st.
Snout
Row 1: (K6, k2tog) 6 times (42 sts).
Row 2 and every foll alt row: Purl.
Row 3: (K5, k2tog) 6 times (36 sts).

Row 5: (K4, k2tog) 6 times (30 sts).
Row 7: (K3, k2tog) 6 times (24 sts).
Work 11 rows in st st.
Nose
Row 1: (K2, k2tog) 6 times (18 sts).
Work 3 rows.
Row 5: (K1, k2tog) 6 times (12 sts).
Row 6: Purl.
Row 7: (K2tog) 6 times (6 sts).
Break yarn leaving a long tail end. Thread the tail end through rem sts, pull tight and fasten off.

Eyebrows (make 2 in pink)
Cast on 4 sts.
Working in g st throughout, inc 1 st at each end of every row to 14 sts.
Cast off.

Back legs (make 2 in A, worked from foot to top of leg)
Cast on 30 sts.
Work 4 rows in st st.
Row 5: K13, ssk, k2tog, k13 (28 sts).
Row 6: P12, p2tog, p2togtbl, p12 (26 sts).
Row 7: K11, ssk, k2tog, k11 (24 sts).
Row 8: P10, p2tog, p2togtbl, p10 (22 sts).
Row 9: K9, ssk, k2tog, k9 (20 sts).
Row 10: Purl.
Work 12 rows in st st.
Top of leg
Row 1: (K1, kfb) 10 times (30 sts).
Row 2: Purl.
Row 3: (K2, kfb) 10 times (40 sts).
Row 4: Purl.
Work 10 rows in st st.
Next row: (K2, k2tog) 10 times (30 sts).
Next row: Purl.
Next row: (K1, k2tog) 10 times (20 sts).
Next row: Purl.

Next row: (K2tog) 10 times (10 sts).
Break yarn leaving a long tail, thread through rem stitches, pull tight and fasten off.

Sole (make 2)
Using B, cast on 4 sts.
Working in g st throughout cont as folls:-
Inc 1 st at each end of every row to 12 sts.
Work 6 rows.
Dec 1 st at each end of every row to 4 sts.
Cast off.

Front arms (make 2)

Using A, cast on 4 sts.

Row 1: Kfb into each st (8 sts).

Row 2 and every foll alt row: Purl.

Row 3: (K1, kfb) 4 times (12 sts).

Row 5: (K2, kfb) 4 times (16 sts).

Work 7 rows in st st.

Next: (K2, k2tog) 4 times (12 sts).

Work 3 rows.

Next: (K1, k2tog) 4 times (8 sts).

Work 5 rows in st st.

Change to B and work 2 rows in st st.

Claws

Row 1: K4, turn and work on these sts only.

Row 2: Purl.

Row 3: (K2tog) twice (2 sts).

Row 4: Purl.

Row 5: K2tog and fasten off. With RS facing, rejoin yarn to last 4 sts.

Work rows 1–5 once more.

Making up

Darn in loose yarn ends.

Body

Sew body front to body back leaving a small opening for stuffing. Stuff firmly and close opening.

Tail

Sew rear seam. Stuff firmly. Position tail over the posterior end of the body, pin and sew firmly in place.

Head

Sew up under seam of head leaving a hole for stuffing. Stuff firmly and close opening.

Facial features

Using A, work two French knots on top of snout (see Finishing Touches page 118). Cut two teardrop-shaped pieces of white felt and stick to head using fabric glue. Sew a button over each piece for eyes. Position each eyebrow above each eye (use photo for reference), with the curved edge pointing upwards. Sew in place with small slip stitches. Cut a strip of white felt approx. ¼in (0.5cm) wide and long enough to fit around the dinosaur's snout. Using a pencil or soluble marker, draw a zigzag line along one long edge. Cut out and stick to the dinosaur's jaws using fabric glue. Use the sewing needle and thread to sew firmly in place with slip stitches.

Legs

Sew rear seam and stuff firmly through the sole. Sew the sole onto the bottom of the leg. Repeat for second leg. Position legs onto the body. Make sure the legs and tail form a balanced triangle shape so your dinosaur will stand unaided. Sew the legs firmly onto the dinosaur using the thread jointing method (see Finishing Touches page 116). Fold the front legs in half lengthwise and sew up leaving the claw end open. Stuff each leg firmly and sew across the end, leaving the claws free.

LOOK!
Allosaurus would never
miss an aerobics class.

These fast-running, two-legged, carnivorous dinosaurs were both smart and deadly predators. Their long, flat snouts held around 80 incredibly sharp, curved teeth many of which were over 1in (2.5cm) in length. They hunted in packs and would eat almost anything, including other dinosaurs.

VELOCIRAPTOR

LOOK!
This Velociraptor is fast and very attractive

Information you'll need

Finished size
Velociraptor measures 9½in (24cm) from head to tail

Materials
Stylecraft Eskimo 100% polyester (98m per 50g)
1 x 50g ball in Silver 5007 (A)
Rico Merino Essentials DK 100% merino (120m per 50g)
1 x 50g ball each in shades:
Silver (98) (B)
Light blue (34) (C)
Jeans (27) (D)
1 pair of 3mm (UK11:US2–3) needles
White and blue felt for eyes and teeth
Fabric glue
Sewing thread and needle
2 small red buttons (approx. ³⁄₁₆in/5mm)
Polyester toy stuffing

Tension
26 sts x 36 rows over 4in (10cm) using 3mm needles and stocking stitch.

DID YOU KNOW?
Velociraptors were very fast and could run up to 40mph (60 km/hr) for short bursts.

How to make Velociraptor

Body back (make 1 in B)
Cast on 6 sts.
Row 1: Kfb into each st (12 sts).
Row 2 and every foll alt row: Purl.
Row 3: (K1, kfb) 6 times (18 sts).
Row 5: (K2, kfb) 6 times (24 sts).
Row 7: (K3, kfb) 6 times (30 sts).
Row 9: (K4, kfb) 6 times (36 sts).
Row 11: (K5, kfb) 6 times (42 sts).
Row 12: Purl.
Work 20 rows in st st.
Row 33: (K5, k2tog) 6 times (36 sts).
Work 3 rows.
Row 37: (K4, k2tog) 6 times (30 sts).
Work 3 rows.
Row 41: (K3, k2tog) 6 times (24 sts).
Work 3 rows.
Row 45: (K2, k2tog) 6 times (18 sts).
Row 46: Purl.
Row 47: (K1, k2tog) 6 times (12 sts).
Row 48: Purl.
Row 49: (K2tog) 6 times (6 sts).
Row 50: Purl.
Cast off.

Body front (make 1 using C and D)
Working in st st and stripe pattern through
work as folls:
Stripe patt
2 rows D/2 rows C.
Cast on 4 sts in D.
Row 1: Kfb into each st (8 sts).
Inc 1 st at each end of next and every foll
alt row to 20 sts.
Work in st st for 11 rows.
Dec 1 st at each end of next and every foll
4th row to 8 sts.
Next row: (K2tog) 4 times (4 sts).
Cast off.

Tail (make 1 using B)
Cast on 32 sts.
Work 12 rows in st st.
Dec 1 st at each end of next and every foll
4th rows to 16 sts.
Work 1 row.
Dec 1 st at each end of next and every foll
alt row to 2 sts.
Next row: K2tog and fasten off.

Tail end (2 pieces)
Under piece
Cast on 2 sts in D.
Working in g st throughout, cont as folls:
Inc 1 st at each end of next and every foll
alt row to 16 sts.
Work 1 row.
Dec 1 st at each end of next and foll 3rd
rows to 2 sts.
Next row: K2tog and fasten off.
Top piece
Cast on 2 sts in A.
Working in st st throughout, work as for
under piece.

Head (make 1 using B)
Cast on 6 sts.
Row 1: Kfb into each st (12 sts).
Row 2 and every foll alt row: Purl.
Row 3: (K1, kfb) 6 times (18 sts).
Row 5: (K2, kfb) 6 times (24 sts).
Row 7: (K3, kfb) 6 times (30 sts).
Row 9: (K4, kfb) 6 times (36 sts).
Row 11: (K5, kfb) 6 times (42 sts).
Work 9 rows in st st.
Snout
Row 1: (K5, k2tog) 6 times (36 sts).
Row 2 and every foll alt rows: Purl.
Row 3: (K4, k2tog) 6 times (30 sts).
Row 5: (K3, k2tog) 6 times (24 sts).
Work 11 rows in st st.
Nose
Row 1: (K2, k2tog) 6 times (18 sts).
Work 3 rows.
Row 5: (K1, k2tog) 6 times (12 sts).
Row 6: Purl.
Row 7: (K2tog) 6 times (6 sts).
Break yarn leaving a long tail end.
Thread the tail end through rem sts, pull
tight and fasten off.

Legs (make 2 using A)
Cast on 6 sts.
Row 1: Kfb into each st (12 sts).
Row 2 and every foll alt row: Purl.
Row 3: (K1, kfb) 6 times (18 sts).
Row 5: (K2, kfb) 6 times (24 sts).
Row 7: (K3, kfb) 6 times (30 sts).
Work 7 rows in st st.
Dec 1 st at each end of next and every foll
4th row to 22 sts.
Work 3 rows in st st.
Next row: (K2tog) 11 times (11 sts).
Next row: Purl.
Next row: K1, (k2tog) 5 times (6 sts).
Cast off.

Feet (make 4 in D)

Cast on 4 sts.

Inc 1 st at each end of next and every foll alt row to 12 sts.

Work 5 rows in st st.

Claws

K4, turn and work on these 4 sts only.

Work 7 rows in st st.

Next row: (K2tog) twice (2 sts).

Next row: (K2tog) and fasten off.

With RS facing, rejoin yarn and knit the next 4 sts, turn and work as for first claw. Rejoin yarn to last set of 4 sts and work as for first and second claw.

Front arms (make 2)

Using A, cast on 4 sts.

Row 1: Kfb into each st (8 sts).

Row 2 and every foll alt row: Purl.

Row 3: (K1, kfb) 4 times (12 sts).

Row 5: (K2, kfb) 4 times (16 sts).

Work 7 rows.

Next row: (K2, k2tog) 4 times (12 sts).

Work 3 rows.

Next row: (K1, k2tog) 4 times (8 sts).

Work 5 rows in st st.

Change to D and work 2 rows in st st.

Claws

Row 1: K4, turn and work on these sts only.

Row 2: Purl.

Row 3: (K2tog) twice (2 sts).

Row 4: Purl.

Row 5: K2tog and fasten off.

With RS facing, rejoin yarn to last 4 sts. Work rows 1–5 once more.

Making up

Darn in loose yarn ends.

Body and head

Sew body front to body back leaving a small opening for stuffing. Stuff firmly and close opening. Sew up under seam of head leaving a hole for stuffing. Stuff firmly and close opening.

Tail and tail end

Sew rear seam. Stuff firmly. Position tail over the posterior end of the body, pin and sew firmly in place. Sew top and under pieces of the tail end together, leaving one side open for stuffing. Stuff firmly. Slip open end over the narrow end of the tail, position it so it is straight and sew up the opening. At the same time, stitch the tail end firmly to the tail itself.

Claws

Take two feet pieces and sew them together, carefully working around each claw. Leave the back of the foot open for stuffing. Stuff firmly and close opening. Repeat for second foot. Sew each foot to the narrow base of each leg.

Legs

Sew rear seam leaving a small hole for stuffing. Stuff firmly and close opening. Repeat for second leg. Fold the front legs in half lengthwise and sew up leaving the claw end open. Stuff each leg firmly and sew across the end, leaving the claws free. Position legs onto the body. Make sure the legs and tail form a balanced triangle shape so your Velociraptor will stand up unaided. Sew the legs on firmly using the thread jointing method (see Finishing Touches page 116).

Facial features

Cut two teardrop-shaped pieces of blue felt for the eyes. Stick these to the head using fabric glue. Sew a button over each piece. For the nostrils, use B to work two French knots on top of snout (see Finishing Touches page 118).

Teeth

Cut a strip of white felt approx ¼in (0.5cm) wide and long enough to fit around the Velociraptor's snout. Using a pencil or soluble marker, draw a zigzag line along one long edge. Cut out and stick to the jaws using fabric glue. Use the sewing needle and thread to sew firmly in place with slip stitches along the straight edge.

Hair

Sew the head firmly on top of the body. Take long strands of yarn A and sew a few long loops to the top of your Velociraptor's head and neck. Secure at base and snip the loops to make tufts.

TROODONS

Small, lightweight and with two long, slender rear legs, Troodons were designed
for running. When they ran, they rotated their huge middle-toe-claw upwards to keep it
out of the way. Troodons were carnivores and ate just about anything they could slash
and tear apart with their sharp teeth and long clawed fingers and toes.

Information you'll need

Finished size

Troodon measures 9in (23cm)
from nose to tail
The carry bag measures 8 x 8in
(20 x 20cm)

Materials (for 3 Troodons)

King Cole Bamboo Cotton 50% bamboo,
50% cotton (220m per 100g)
1 x 100g ball each in shades:
Peacock (531) (A)
Green (533) (B)
Fuchsia (536) (C)
Black (534) (D)
1 pair of 3mm (UK11:US2–3) needles
6 small green buttons (approx. ³⁄₁₆in/5mm)
Pink felt for footprint motif
Sewing needle and thread
19½in (50cm) green ribbon

Tension

26 sts x 36 rows over 4in (10cm) using
3mm needles and stocking stitch.

LOOK!
You can keep your
pet Troodons in this
handy carry bag!

How to make Troodons

Body: worked nose to tail (make 1 of each in A, C and B)

Cast on 6 sts.
Row 1: Kfb into each st (12 sts).
Row 2 and every foll alt row: Purl.
Row 3: (K1, kfb) 6 times (18 sts).
Row 4: Purl.
Work 4 rows in st st.
Row 9: (K1, k2tog) 6 times (12 sts).
Row 10: Purl.
Work 2 rows in st st.
Row 13: (K1, k2tog) 4 times (8 sts).
Inc 1 st at each end of next and every foll row to 28 sts.
Work 10 rows in st st.
Dec 1 st at each end of next and every foll alt rows to 2 sts.
Next row: P2tog and fasten off.

Arms (make 2 in chosen colour)

Cast on 5 sts.
Beg with a K row, work in st st for 16 rows.
Cast off.

Back legs (make 2 in chosen colour)

Cast on 6 sts.
Row 1: Kfb into each st (12 sts).
Row 2 and every foll alt row: Purl.
Row 3: (K1, kfb) 6 times (18 sts).
Row 4: Purl.
Work 4 rows in st st.
Row 9: (K1, k2tog) 6 times (12 sts).
Row 10: Purl.
Work 2 rows in st st.
Row 13: (K1, k2tog) 4 times (8 sts).
Row 14: Purl.
Work 12 rows in st st.
Dec 1 st at each end of next and every foll alt rows to 4 sts.
Break yarn leaving a long tail.
Thread yarn through rem sts, draw tight and fasten off.

Making up

Darn in loose yarn ends. Sew under seam on body piece leaving a small hole for stuffing. Stuff firmly and close opening. Sew seam of back legs leaving a small opening. Stuff firmly and close opening. Position legs onto sides of your Troodon. Sew in place using thread jointing (see Finishing Touches page 116). Position arms and sew in place. Sew buttons onto sides of head for eyes.

DID YOU KNOW?

Troodons may have been the smartest dinosaurs, since they had the largest brain in proportion to their body weight.

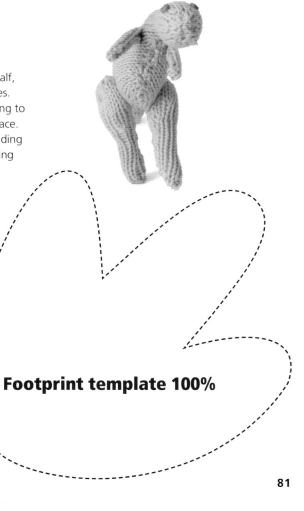

Making the carry bag

Using D, cast on 44 sts.
Work 6 rows in st st.

Turning rows for casing

Knit 2 rows.
Change to A and work in stripe patt as set below and st st, cont as folls:
6 rows A/2 rows D.
Rep these 8 rows 14 times.
Change to A and work 6 rows.
Change to D.

Turning rows for casing

Knit 2 rows.
Work 6 rows in st st.
Cast off.

Making up

Darn in loose yarn ends. Fold bag in half, matching top and bottom casing edges. Sew one side seam. Fold over the casing to the WS of the bag and slip stitch in place. Now sew the remaining side seam, ending just below the casing so that an opening is left for the ribbon. Cut a piece of ribbon 21in (53cm) long, thread it through the casing and tie the ends in a knot. Cut out a dinosaur footprint in pink felt using the template. Pin onto the front of bag and stitch in place using small back stitches (see Finishing Touches page 119). Place Troodons in bagand pull ribbon tight to close.

Footprint template 100%

Spinosaurus or 'spiny lizard', were the largest meat-eating dinosaurs at an enormous 55ft (17m). Their extremely long crocodile-like snouts and large array of teeth were used to eat plant-eating dinosaurs and fish. These giant carnivore's most striking feature was the tall sail running down their backs, which may have been used to disperse heat, to attract mates or to intimidate other dinosaurs.

SPINOSAURUS

Information you'll need

Finished size
Spinosaurus measures 18in (46cm) from nose to tail

Materials
Artesano Superwash Merino DK
100% merino (120m per 50g)
2 x 50g balls in shade Sea blue (1291) (A)
1 x 50g ball in shade Lime green (6315) (B)
1 pair of 3mm (UK11:US2–3) needles
Yellow and white felt for eyes and teeth
Sewing needle and white thread
2 small red buttons (approx. $\frac{3}{16}$in/5mm)
Fabric glue
Polyester toy stuffing

Tension
26 sts x 36 rows over 4in (10cm) using 3mm needles and stocking stitch.

How to make Spinosaurus

Body: worked tail to head (make 1)

Using A, cast on 3 sts.
Row 1 (WS): Purl.
Working in st st, inc 1 st at each end of next and every foll alt row to 17 sts.
Work 1 row. Inc 1 st at each end of next and every foll 4th row to 33 sts.
Work 13 rows in st st.

Belly

Row 1: Kfb, k14, kfb, k1, kfb, k14, kfb (37 sts).
Row 2: Pfb, p17, k1, p17, pfb (39 sts).
Row 3: Kfb, k17, kfb, k1, kfb, k17, kfb (43 sts).
Row 4: Pfb, p20, k1, p20, pfb (45 sts).
Row 5: Kfb, k20, kfb, k1, kfb, k20, kfb (49 sts).
Row 6: Pfb, p23, k1, p23, pfb (51 sts).
Row 7: Kfb, k23, kfb, k1, kfb, k23, kfb (55 sts).
Row 8: Purl.
Work 8 rows in st st. Dec 1 st at each end of next and foll 4th rows (51 sts). Work 1 row. Dec 1 st at each end of next and every foll alt rows to 37 sts. Work 1 row.

Neck

Row 1: Ssk, k14, ssk, k1, k2tog, k14, k2tog (33 sts).
Row 2: P16, k1, p16.
Row 3: Ssk, k12, ssk, k1, k2tog, k12, k2tog (29 sts).
Row 4: P14, k1, p14.
Row 5: Ssk, k10, ssk, k1, k2tog, k10, k2tog (25 sts).
Row 6: P12, k1, p12.
Row 7: Ssk, k8, ssk, k1, k2tog, k8, k2tog (21 sts).
Row 8: Purl. Work 4 rows in st st.

Head

Row 1: K9, kfb, k1, kfb, k9 (23 sts).
Row 2: P10, pfb, k1, pfb, p10 (25 sts).
Row 3: K11, kfb, k1, kfb, k11 (27 sts).
Row 4: P12, pfb, k1, pfb, p12 (29 sts).

Row 5: K13, kfb, k1, kfb, k13 (31 sts).
Row 6: P14, pfb, k1, pfb, p14 (33 sts).
Work 6 rows in st st.
Row 13: K14, ssk, k1, k2tog, k14 (31 sts).
Row 14: P13, p2tog, k1, p2togtbl, p13 (29 sts).
Row 15: K12, ssk, k1, k2tog, k12 (27 sts).
Row 16: Purl.
Row 17: Knit.
Row 18: P2tog, P to end of row (26 sts).

Jaws

Row 1: K20, turn, leave rem 6 sts on a holder.
Row 2: P13 sts, turn, leave rem 7 sts on holder.
Working on these 13 sts only, work 6 rows in st st. Dec 1 st at each end of next and every foll 4th row to 9 sts. Work 1 row. Dec 1 st at each end of next and every foll alt rows until 3 sts rem. Work 1 row.
Next row: Sl1, k2tog, psso and fasten off. For lower jaw, slide both sets of stitches from the stitch holders onto 1 needle. Make sure they line up without twisting and the RS is facing you for the next row. You want a row of 13 sts which lay parallel below the top jaw. Work 6 rows in st st. Dec 1 st at each end of next and every foll 4th row to 9 sts. Work 1 row. Dec 1 st each end of next and every foll alt rows until 3 sts rem. Work 1 row.
Next row: Sl1, k2tog, psso and fasten off.

Mouth gusset (make 1 in B)

Using B, cast on 3 sts. Beg with a K row, and working in st st throughout, cont as folls:- Inc 1 st at each end of next and foll alt rows to 9 sts. Work 1 row. Inc 1 st at each end of next and every foll 4th row to 13 sts. Work 15 rows in st st. Dec 1 st at each end of next and every foll 4th row to 9 sts. Work 1 row. Dec 1 st at each end of next and every foll alt rows to 3 sts.
Next row: Sl1, k2tog, psso and fasten off.

Back legs: worked from foot to top of leg (make 2)

Using A, cast on 30 sts. Beg with a K row, work 4 rows in st st.
Row 5: K13, ssk, k2tog, k13 (28 sts).
Row 6: P12, p2tog, p2togtbl, p12 (26 sts).
Row 7: K11, ssk, k2tog, k11 (24 sts).
Row 8: P10, p2tog, p2togtbl, p10 (22 sts).
Row 9: K9, ssk, k2tog, k9 (20 sts).
Row 10: Purl. Work 4 rows in B. Work 4 rows in A. Work 4 rows in B. Change to A.

Top of leg

Row 1: (K1, kfb) 10 times (30 sts).
Row 2: Purl.
Row 3: (K2, kfb) 10 times (40 sts).
Row 4: Purl. Work 10 rows in st st.
Next row: (K2, k2tog) 10 times (30 sts).
Next row: Purl.

Next row: (K1, k2tog) 10 times (20 sts).
Next row: Purl.
Next row: (K2tog) 10 times (10 sts). Break yarn leaving a long tail, thread through rem stitches, pull tight and fasten off.

Sole (make 2)
Using B, cast on 4 sts. Working in g st throughout cont as folls:- Inc 1 st at each end of every row to 12 sts. Work 6 rows. Dec 1 st at each end of every row to 4 sts. Cast off.

Front legs (make 2)
Using B, cast on 4 sts.
Row 1: Kfb into each st (8 sts).
Row 2 and every foll alt row: Purl.
Row 3: (K1, kfb) 4 times (12 sts).
Row 5: (K2, kfb) 4 times (16 sts). Work 7 rows straight.
Next row: (K2, k2tog) 4 times (12 sts). Work 3 rows.
Next row: (K1, k2tog) 4 times (8 sts). Work 5 rows in st st. Change to A and work 2 rows in st st.
Claws
Row 1: K4, turn and work on these sts only.
Row 2: Purl.
Row 3: (K2tog) twice (2 sts).
Row 4: Purl.
Row 5: K2tog and fasten off.
With RS facing, rejoin yarn to last 4 sts. Work rows 1–5 once more.

Spiny sail
Side 1
Using B, cast on 6 sts.
Working in st st and stripe patt of 4 rows B/4 rows A, cont as folls:- Inc 1 st at the end of next and every foll alt row to 14 sts. Work 9 rows without shaping, ending with RS facing for next row. Dec 1 st at end of next and every foll alt rows to 6 sts. Work 1 row. Cast off.

Side 2
Using B, cast on 6 sts.
Working in st st and stripe patt of 4 rows B/4 rows A, cont as folls:- Inc 1 st at beg of next and every foll alt row to 14 sts. Work 9 rows without shaping, ending with RS facing for next row. Dec 1 st at beg of next and every foll alt row to 6 sts. Work 1 row. Cast off.

Making up
Darn in loose yarn ends. Sew up belly seam on body and stuff through mouth firmly, leaving the head unstuffed for the moment. Using the purl side of the mouth gusset as the RS, pin the gusset inside the jaws and stitch around each edge leaving a small opening for stuffing. Finish stuffing the head and body and close opening.

Legs
Sew rear seam and stuff firmly through the sole. Sew the sole onto the bottom of the leg. Repeat for second leg. Position legs onto the body. Make sure the legs and tail form a balanced triangle shape so your Spinosaurus will stand up unaided. Sew the legs on firmly using the thread jointing method (see Finishing Touches page 116). Fold the front legs in half lengthwise and sew up leaving the claw end open. Stuff each leg firmly and sew across the end, leaving the claws free.

Facial features
Cut 2 teardrop shapes from yellow felt for the eyes and stick in place with fabric glue. Sew a small button on top of each. Using A, sew 2 French knots (see Finishing Touches page 118) on top of the top jaw for the nostrils (refer to photo).

Teeth
Cut a strip of white felt approx ½in (1cm) wide. Make sure it is long enough to wrap around the top edge of the Spinosaurus' jaws. Draw a zig-zag line through the centre of the strip with a pencil or soluble marker and cut this line. You will have 2 zig-zag strips, each with a straight edge. Dab the straight edges with fabric glue. Stick in place along top and bottom edges of jaw. Use the sewing thread and needle to stitch firmly in place along the straight edge.

Spiny sail
Place both pieces together and sew together along curved edge. Using B, PUK 30 sts along the curved edge working through both thicknesses. Turn and work Picot Cast off as folls: Cast off 3 sts, (cast on 2 sts in the stitch on your LH needle, cast off 4 sts) rep brackets to last stitch. Fasten off. Stuff the Sail firmly through the bottom opening. Pin the sail to the Spinosaurus' back and stitch firmly in position.

PLESIOSAUR

These large, marine reptiles ranged in size from 8–46ft (2.5–14m) long. They had four paddle-like flippers, sharp teeth in strong jaws and short, pointed tails. Plesiosaurs lived in the oceans and ate fish and other marine animals.

Information you'll need

Finished size
Plesiosaur measures 10¾in (27cm)

Materials
Artesano Merino Superwash DK
100% merino (112m per 50g)
1 x 50g ball each in shades:
Teal (5167) (A)
Baby green (8361) (B)
1 pair of 3mm (UK11:US2–3) needles
Approx 1¼ x ¼in (35 x 4mm)
semi-cupped silver sequins
Small piece of white felt for eyes
2 small brown buttons (approx. ³⁄₁₆in/5mm)
Fabric glue
Sewing thread and needle
Polyester toy stuffing

Tension
26 sts x 36 rows to 4in (10cm) over st st
using 3mm needles.
Use larger or smaller needles if necessary
to obtain correct tension.

How to make Plesiosaur

Upper body: worked head to tail (make 1)

Using A, cast on 3 sts.
Row 1: Kfb, k1, kfb (5 sts).
Row 2 and every foll alt row: Purl.
Row 3: Kfb, kfb, k1, kfb, kfb (9 sts).
Row 5: Kfb, k2, kfb, k1, kfb, k2, kfb (13 sts).
Row 7: Kfb, k4, kfb, k1, kfb, k4, kfb (17 sts).
Row 9: Kfb, k6, kfb, k1, kfb, k6, kfb (21 sts).
Row 11: Kfb, k8, kfb, k1, kfb, k8, kfb (25 sts).
Dec 1 st at each end of next and foll alt rows to 21 sts.
Dec 1 st at each end of every row to 11 sts.
Work 10 rows in st st.
Inc 1 st at each end of next and every foll row to 31 sts.
Inc 1 st at each end of next and every foll alt row to 37 sts.
Purl 1 row.
Work 20 rows in st st.
Dec 1 st at each end of next and every foll alt rows to 31 sts and then on every row to 9 sts.
Work 6 rows in st st.
Dec 1 st at each end of next and every foll alt rows to 3 sts.
Next row: Purl.
Next row: Sl1, k2tog, psso. Fasten off.

Belly: worked head to tail (make 1)

Using B, cast on 3 sts.
Row 1: Kfb, k1, kfb (5 sts).
Row 2 and every foll alt row: Purl.
Row 3: K1, kfb, k1, kfb, k1 (7 sts).
Row 5: K2, kfb, k1, kfb, k2 (9 sts).
Row 7: K3, kfb, k1, kfb, k3 (11 sts).
Dec 1 st at each end of next and foll alt row (7 sts).

Work 11 rows in st st.
Inc 1 st at each end of next and every foll row to 29 sts and then on every alt row to 35 sts.
Work 21 rows in st st.
Dec 1 st at each end of next and every foll row to 7 sts.
Work 7 rows in st st.
Dec 1 st at each end of next and every foll alt row to 3 sts.
Next row: Purl.
Next row: Sl1, k2tog, psso. Fasten off.

Back paddles (make 2 in A and 2 in B)

Cast on 3 sts.
Row 1: Kfb, k1, kfb (5 sts).
Row 2 and every foll alt row: Purl.
Row 3: Kfb, p1, k1, p1, kfb (7 sts).
Row 5: Kfb, k1, (p1, k1) twice, kfb (9 sts).
Row 7: Kfb, p1, (k1, p1) 3 times, kfb (11 sts).

Row 9: P1, (k1, p1) 5 times.
Row 11: Kfb, (k1, p1) 4 times, k1, kfb (13 sts).
Row 13: K1, (p1, k1) 6 times.
Row 15: Kfb, (p1, k1) 5 times, p1, kfb (15 sts).
Row 17: (P1, k1) 7 times, p1.
Row 19: Kfb, (k1, p1) 6 times, k1, kfb (17 sts).
Row 21: (K1, p1) 8 times, k1.
Row 22: Purl.*
Rep rows 21 and 22 once more.
Keeping to rib pattern as set, dec 1 st at each end of next and every foll 4th row to 7 sts.
Work 9 rows in rib pattern.
Cast off.

Front paddles (make 2 in A and 2 in B)

Work as for back paddles to*.
Rep rows 21 and 22 twice more.
Keeping to rib pattern as set, dec 1 st at each end of next and every foll 4th row to 7 sts.
Work 9 rows in rib pattern.
Cast off.

Making up

Sew in loose yarn ends. Sew upper to belly leaving a small opening for stuffing. Stuff firmly and close opening. Sew upper and lower parts of all paddles leaving a small opening for stuffing. Stuff firmly and close opening. Position paddles to side of body and sew firmly in place. Sew sequins randomly over the plesiosaur's back with sewing thread. Cut two teardrop shapes of white felt for eyes; stick in place using fabric glue. Sew a button on top of each piece.

DID YOU KNOW?
Plesiosaurs swallowed small stones to help grind up the food in their stomachs.

Ichthyosaurus were streamlined marine reptiles with big eyes, strong jaws and sharp teeth. They were fast, powerful swimmers, using their four crescent-shaped fins to stabilize themselves in the water and their fish-like tails to propel themselves forward.

ICHTHYOSAURUS

Information you'll need

Finished size

Ichthyosaurus measures 19in (48cm)
from head to tail

Materials

Sirdar Big Softie 51% wool, 49% acrylic
(45m per 50g)
2 x 50g balls in Vivid (345) (A)
2 x 50g balls in Souffle (333) (B)
1 x 50g ball in Mitten (341) (C)
1 pair of 9mm (UK00:US13) needles
2 stitch holders or safety pins
Small pieces of blue and white felt
for eyes and teeth
Sewing thread and needle
2 buttons for eyes (approx. ⁹⁄₁₆in/15mm)
Fabric glue
Polyester toy stuffing

Tension

10 sts and 14 rows over 4in (10cm)
over st st using 9mm needles.
Use larger or smaller needles if
necessary to obtain correct tension.

DID YOU KNOW?

Ichthyosaurus could
not move about
on land.

How to make Ichthyosaurus

Body: worked tail to jaws (make 1)

Using A, cast on 6 sts.
Row 1: Kfb into each st (12 sts).
Row 2 and every foll alt rows: Purl.
Row 3: (K1, kfb) 6 times (18 sts).
Row 5: (K2, kfb) 6 times (24 sts).
Row 6: Purl.
Change to B and work 2 rows in st st.
Change to C.
Inc 1 st at each end of next row (26 sts).
Work 3 rows in st st.
Change to B.
Inc 1 st at each end of next row (28 sts).
Work 1 row.
Change to A.
Work 2 rows in st st.
Inc 1 st at each end of next row (30 sts).
Work 3 rows in st st.
Change to B and work 2 rows.
Change to C and work 4 rows.
Change to B and work 2 rows.
Change to A and work 6 rows.
Change to B, dec 1 st at each end of next and every foll alt rows to 24 sts.
Work 5 rows in st st, ending with RS facing for next row.

Divide for jaws

Row 1: K18, turn and leave rem 6 sts on a holder.
Row 2: P12, turn and leave rem 6 sts on a holder.
Work 4 rows on these 12 sts only.
Dec 1 st at each end of next and every foll alt row to 4 sts.
Work 5 rows in st st.
Next row: (K2tog) twice.
Next row: K2tog and fasten off.
For lower jaw, slide both sets of stitches from the stitch holders onto 1 needle. Make sure they line up without twisting and the RS is facing you for the next row. You want a row of 12 sts which lay parallel below the top jaw.
Work 4 rows on these 12 sts.
Then dec 1 st at each end of next and every foll alt row to 4 sts.
Work 5 rows in st st.
Next row: (K2tog) twice.
Next row: K2tog and fasten off.

Mouth gusset (make 1)

Using C, cast on 2 sts.
Row 1: Kfb into each st (4 sts).
Beg with a P row, work 3 rows in st st.
Inc 1 st at each end of next and every foll alt row to 12 sts.
Work 7 rows in st st.
Then dec 1 st at each end of next and every foll alt row to 4 sts.
Work 5 rows in st st.
Next row: (K2tog) twice.
Next row: K2tog and fasten off.

Top fin (make 2)

Using A, cast on 11 sts.
Working in g st throughout, cont as folls:-
Knit 1 row.
Dec 1 st at each end of next and every foll alt rows to 3 sts.
Next row: Sl1, k2tog and psso and fasten off.

Front paddles
(make 2 in A and 2 in B)
Cast on 4 sts.
Beg with a K row, working in st st, inc 1 st at each end of next and every foll alt rows to 12 sts.
Purl 1 row.
Dec 1 st at each end of next and every foll alt rows to 4 sts.
Next row: (K2tog) twice (2 sts).
Next row: K2tog and fasten off.

Back paddles
(Make 2 in A and 2 in B)
Cast on 4 sts.
Beg with a K row, working in st st, inc 1 st at each end of next and every foll alt rows to 10 sts.
Purl 1 row.
Dec 1 st at each end of next and every foll row to 4 sts.
Next row: (K2tog) twice.
Next row: K2tog and fasten off.

Tail
(make 2)
Using B, cast on 12 sts.
Beg with a K row, work 2 rows in st st.
Inc 1 st at each end of next row (14 sts).
Next row: Purl.
Change to A and work 4 rows in st st.
Divide for tail fins
Row 1: K7, turn and work on these sts only.
Work 5 rows in st st.
Dec 1 st at each end of next and every foll alt rows to 3 sts.
Next row: Purl.
Next row: Sl1, k2tog, psso and fasten off.
With RS facing, rejoin yarn to rem 7 sts and repeat tail fin shapings to match first.

Making up
Darn in loose yarn ends.

Body and head
Sew up belly seam on body and stuff through mouth firmly, leaving the head unstuffed for the moment. Pin the mouth gusset inside the jaws and stitch around each edge leaving a small opening for stuffing. Finish stuffing the head and body and close opening.

Fins and paddles
Pin both pieces of the top fin together; sew around top two edges. Stuff firmly through the open bottom seam. Position fin onto the Ichthyosaurus' back and stitch in place. Sew seams of all four paddles, leaving a small opening for stuffing. Stuff each paddle firmly and close the opening. Position paddles according to photo and stitch firmly in place.

Tail
Sew both parts of the tail together leaving the cast-on edge open. Stuff firmly, slide onto the base of the Ichthyosaurus and stitch in place.

Facial features
Cut two teardrop shapes in blue felt for the eyes and glue onto sides of head. Sew a button on top of each. For the teeth, cut four zig-zag strips of white felt long enough to line the edges of the upper and lower edges of the Ichthyosaurus' jaws. Stick in place with fabric glue, then using sewing thread, stitch around the top edge with small neat stitches to keep the teeth fully secure.

MESOSAURUS

Mesosaurus, meaning middle lizard, were small, freshwater reptiles. They were light in build with an elongated head and a flattened tail, perfect for swimming. Their flipper-like feet would have also helped propel them through the water. Mesosaurus probably ate fish and shrimp, catching them in their mouths.

Information you'll need

Finished size

Mesosaurus measures 19¼in (49cm) from head to tail

Materials

Stylecraft Life DK 75% acrylic, 25% wool (298m per 100g)
1 x 100g ball each in shades:
Claret (2310) (A)
Raspberry Marl (2347) (B)
1 pair of 3mm (UK11: US2–3) needles
2 stitch holders or safety pins
Square of white felt for eyes and teeth
Sewing thread and needle
2 small buttons for eyes (approx. ³⁄₁₆in/5mm)
Fabric glue
Polyester toy stuffing

Tension

26 sts x 36 rows over 4in (10cm) over st st using 3mm needles.
Use larger or smaller needles if necessary to obtain correct tension.

How to make Mesosaurus

Body: worked from tail to nose (make 1)

Using B, cast on 3 sts.

Tail

Row 1: Kfb in each st (6 sts).

Row 2 and every foll alt row: Purl.

Row 3: Kfb in each stitch (12 sts).

Row 5: (K1, kfb) 6 times (18 sts).

Row 7: (K2, kfb) 6 times (24 sts).

Cont in stocking stitch until work meas 5in (13cm) ending with a P row.

Body

Next row: (K3, kfb) 6 times (30 sts). Work 3 rows.

Next row: (K4, kfb) 6 times (36 sts). Work 3 rows.

Next row: (K5, kfb) 6 times (42 sts). Work 3 rows.

Next row: (K6, kfb) 6 times (48 sts). Work straight until work meas 12in (30cm), ending on a P row.

Next row: (K6, k2tog) 6 times (42 sts). Work 3 rows.

Next row: (K5, k2tog) 6 times (36 sts). Work 3 rows.

Next row: (K4, k2tog) 6 times (30 sts). Work 3 rows.

Next row: (K3, k2tog) 6 times (24 sts). Work 9 rows straight.

Head

Row 1: (K3, kfb) 6 times (30 sts).

Row 2: Purl.

Row 3: (K4, kfb) 6 times (36 sts). Work 9 rows straight.

Divide for jaws

Row 1: K27, turn and leave rem 9 sts on a holder.

Row 2: P18, turn and leave rem 9 sts on holder. Work 2 rows on these 18 sts only. Dec 1 st at each end of next and every foll alt rows to 6 sts. Work 9 rows straight. Dec 1 st at each end of next row (4 sts). Work 1 row.

Next row: (K2tog) twice (2 sts).

Next row: K2tog and fasten off. For lower jaw, slide both sets of stitches from the stitch holders onto 1 needle. Make sure they line up without twisting and the RS is facing you for the next row. You want a row of 18 sts which lay parallel below the top jaw. Work 2 rows straight on these 18 sts. Dec 1 st at each end of next and every foll alt rows to 6 sts. Work 9 rows straight. Dec 1 st at each end of next row (4 sts). Work 1 row.

Next row: (K2tog) twice (2 sts).

Next row: K2tog and fasten off.

Mouth gusset (make 1)

Using A, cast on 4 sts.

Row 1: Kfb into each st (8 sts).

Row 2 and every foll alt rows: Purl.

Row 3: Kfb, k2, kfb (6 sts). Work 9 rows in stocking stitch. Inc 1 st at each end of next and every foll alt rows to 18 sts.
Work 3 rows. Dec 1 st at each end of next and every foll alt rows to 6 sts. Work 9 rows straight. Dec 1 st at each end of next row (4 sts).

Next row: Purl.

Next row: (K2tog) twice (2 sts).

Next row: K2tog and fasten off.

Top fin (make 1)

Using A, cast on 55 sts. Beg working in moss stitch as folls:

Row 1: * K1, p1, rep from * to last st, k1. Rep this row once more. Then keeping to patt, inc 1 st at each end of the next 6 rows (67 sts).
Cast off in moss stitch.

Bottom fin (make 1)

Using A, cast on 41 sts. Beg working in moss stitch as folls:

Row 1: * K1, p1 rep from * to last st, k1. Rep this row once more. Then keeping to patt, inc 1 st at each end of the next 6 rows (53 sts).
Cast off in moss stitch.

Back legs (make 2)

Using A, cast on 6 sts.

Row 1: Kfb into each st (12 sts).

Row 2 and every foll alt row: Purl.

Row 3: (K1, kfb) 6 times (18 sts).

Row 5: (K2, kfb) 6 times (24 sts).
Change to B and working in stripe patt of 4 rows B/4 rows A cont as folls:-
Work 9 rows in st st.

Next row: (K2, k2tog) 6 times (18 sts). Work 3 rows.

Next row: (K1, k2tog) 6 times (12 sts). Work 5 rows. Dec 1 st each end of next and every foll alt rows to 8 sts.
Work 3 rows.

Claws

Row 1: K4, turn and work on these 4 sts only.

Row 2: Purl.

Row 3: (K2tog) twice (2 sts).

Row 4: Purl.

Row 5: K2tog and fasten off. With RS facing, rejoin yarn to rem 4 sts and rep rows 1–5 as for first claw.

Front legs (make 2)

Using A, cast on 4 sts. Working in stripe patt cont as folls;

Row 1: Kfb into each st (8 sts).

Row 2 and every foll alt row: Purl.

Row 3: (K1, kfb) 4 times (12 sts).

Row 5: (K2, kfb) 4 times (16 sts). Change to B and stripe patt of 4 rows B/4 rows A cont as folls:- Work 7 rows straight.

Next row: (K2, k2tog) 4 times (12 sts). Work 3 rows.

Next row: (K1, k2tog) 4 times (8 sts). Work 5 rows.

Claws

Row 1: K4, turn and work on these sts only.

Row 2: Purl.

Row 3: (K2tog) twice (2 sts).

Row 4: Purl.

Row 5: K2tog and fasten off.
With RS facing, rejoin yarn to last 4 sts. Work rows 1–5 once more.

Making up

Body and head

Darn in loose yarn ends. Sew up belly seam on body and stuff through mouth firmly, leaving the head unstuffed for the moment. Pin the mouth gusset inside the jaws and stitch around each edge leaving a small opening for stuffing. Finish stuffing the head and body and close opening.

Fins

Sew on the top and bottom tail fins, joining the mitres at the end of the tail.

Legs

Fold the legs in half lengthwise and sew up leaving the claw end open. Stuff each leg firmly and sew across the end, leaving the claws free. Position legs onto the body and sew firmly in place.

Facial features

Cut two teardrop shapes in white felt for the eyes and glue onto sides of head. Sew a red button on top of each. For the teeth, cut four zig-zag strips of white felt long enough to line the edges of the upper and lower edges of the mesosaurus' jaws. Stick in place with fabric glue then using sewing thread, stitch around the top edge with small neat stitches to keep the teeth fully secure.

DID YOU KNOW?
Mesosaurus may seldom have ventured onto land.

The Pterodactyls were a group of flying reptiles that ranged in size from a wingspan of a few inches to over 40ft (12m). They were lightly built with hollow bones, long, curved necks, and small bodies. They had large brains and good eyesight.

PTERODACTYL

Information you'll need

Finished size
Pterodactyl measures 7in (18cm) in height

Materials
Rico Essentials Merino DK
100% merino (120m per 50g)
1 x 50g ball each in shades:
Magenta (10) (A)
Mauve (20) (B)
Silver grey (98) (C)
1 pair of 3mm (UK11: US2–3) needles
Fabric glue
2 small green buttons (approx. ³⁄₁₆in/5mm)
Small piece of white felt for eyes
Sewing thread and needle
Polyester toy stuffing

Tension
26 sts and 36 rows to 10cm (4in) over
st st using 3mm needles.

DID YOU KNOW?
Pterodactyls ate fish from
the surface of the oceans,
as well as scavenging dead
animals on land.

How to make Pterodactyl

Wings (make 1 in B and 1 in C)

Cast on 3 sts.
Row 1: Kfb, k1, kfb (5 sts).
Row 2: P2, k1, p2.
Row 3: Kfb, k to last st, kfb (7 sts).
Row 4: P3, k1, p3.
Row 5: As Row 3 (9 sts).
Row 6: P4, k1, p4.
Row 7: As Row 3 (11 sts).
Row 8: P5, k1, p5.
Row 9: As Row 3 (13 sts).
Row 10: P6, k1, p6.
Row 11: As Row 3 (15 sts).
Row 12: P7, k1, p7 **.
Row 13: K to last st, kfb (16 sts).
Row 14: P8, k1, p7.
Row 15: As Row 13 (17 sts).
Row 16: P9, k1, p7. Rep the last 2 rows increasing 1 st at end of the RS row to 25 sts and keeping the K st on the WS row as set.

Next row: Knit.
Next row: P17, k1, p7. Rep these last 2 rows 11 times (22 rows in total). Work 2 rows in garter stitch.
Next row: Knit.
Next row: P17, k1, p7.
Rep these last 2 rows 11 times (22 rows in total).
Next row: K to last 2 sts, k2tog (23 sts).
Next row: P16, k1, p7. Rep the last 2 rows decreasing at end of the RS rows to 15 sts and keeping the K st on the WS row as set. Dec 1 st at each end of the next and every foll alt row to 3 sts keeping the K st on the WS row as set.
Next row: Sl1, k2tog, psso and fasten off.

Tail (make 1 in B)

Cast on 3 sts. Working in g st, inc 1 st each end of next and every foll row to 11 sts. Work 2 rows. Dec 1 st at each end of next and every foll row to 3 sts. Now work in st st until tail meas 5in (13cm), ending on a WS row.
Cast off.

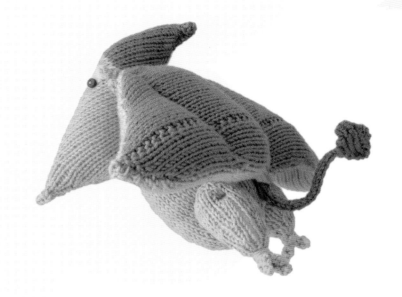

Body (make 1)

Using A, cast on 3 sts. Working in st st and stripe pattern of 2 rows A and 2 rows C, cont as folls:-

Row 1: Kfb into each st (6 sts).
Row 2 and every foll alt rows: Purl.
Row 3: As row 1 (12 sts).
Row 5: (K1, kfb) 6 times (18 sts).
Row 7: (K2, kfb) 6 times (24 sts).
Row 9: (K3, kfb) 6 times (30 sts).
Row 11: (K4, kfb) 6 times (36 sts).
Row 13: (K5, kfb) 6 times (42 sts).
Row 14: Purl. Work 18 rows straight.

Top

Row 1: (K5, k2tog) 6 times (36 sts).
Row 2 and every foll alt row: Purl.
Row 3: (K4, k2tog) 6 times (30 sts).
Row 5: (K3, k2tog) 6 times (24 sts).
Row 7: (K2, k2tog) 6 times (18 sts).
Row 9: (K1, k2tog) 6 times (12 sts).
Row 11: (K2tog) 6 times (6 sts). Break yarn leaving a long tail, thread through rem sts and pull tight.

Head (make 1)

Using B, work as given for wings to **, cont in this way until there are 25 sts. Change to C.

Row 1: Kfb, k9, ssk, k1, k2tog, k9, kfb (25 sts).
Row 2: Pfb, p11, k1, p11, pfb (27 sts).
Row 3: Kfb, k10, ssk, k1, k2tog, k10, kfb (27 sts).
Row 4: Pfb, p12, k1, p12, pfb (29 sts).
Row 5: Kfb, k11, ssk, k1, k2tog, k11, kfb (29 sts).
Row 6: Pfb, p13, k1, p13, pfb (31 sts).
Row 7: Kfb, k12, ssk, k1, k2tog, k12, kfb (31 sts).

Row 8: P15, k1, p15 (31 sts). Rep rows 7 and 8 once more.
Row 11: K13, ssk, k1, k2tog, k13 (29 sts).
Row 12: P14, k1, p14.
Row 13: K12, ssk, k1, k2tog, k12 (27 sts).
Row 14: P13, k1, p13.
Row 15: K11, ssk, k1, k2tog, k11 (25 sts).
Row 16: P12, k1, p12.
Row 17: Ssk, k8, ssk, k1, k2tog, k8, k2tog (21 sts).
Row 18: P10, k1, p10. Work 4 rows straight keeping the K st on the WS row as set. Dec 1 st at each end of next and every foll alt rows to 3 sts.
Next row: Sl1, k2tog, psso. Fasten off.

Legs (make 2)

Using A, cast on 6 sts. Working in stocking stitch and stripe pattern of 2 rows A and 2 rows C throughout, cont as folls:-

Row 1: Kfb into each st (12 sts).

Row 2 and every foll alt row: Purl.

Row 3: (K1, kfb) 6 times (18 sts).

Row 5: (K2, kfb) 6 times (24 sts). Work 3 rows.

Row 9: (K2, k2tog) 6 times (18 sts). Work 3 rows.

Row 13: (K1, k2tog) 6 times (12 sts). Work 3 rows.

Row 17: (K1, k2tog) 4 times (8 sts). Work 3 rows.

Claws

Row 1: K4, turn and work on these 4 sts.

Row 2: Purl.

Row 3: (K2tog) twice (2 sts).

Row 4: Purl.

Row 5: K2tog. Fasten off. With RS facing rejoin yarn to rem 4 sts and work rows 1–5 once more.

Arms (make 2)

Using A, cast on 10 sts. Beg with a K row, work in st st for 14 rows. Dec 1 st at each end of next row (8 sts).

Next row: Purl.

Claws

Row 1: K4, turn and work on these 4 sts.

Row 2: Purl.

Row 3: (K2tog) twice (2 sts).

Row 4: Purl.

Row 5: K2tog. Fasten off. With RS facing, rejoin yarn to rem 4 sts and work rows 1–5 once more.

Making up

Darn in all loose yarn ends.

Wings

With RS facing, sew both parts of the wings together leaving a small hole for turning and stuffing. Turn RS out and stuff firmly. Close opening. Using contrast yarn, run 3 lines of back stitch through all layers: one through the centre garter stitch seam, and one either side running from the wing corners downwards (refer to photo).

Body and head

Sew rear seam leaving a small hole for stuffing. Stuff firmly and close opening.

Legs and arms

Fold the legs and arms in half lengthwise and sew up leaving the claw end open. Stuff each leg and sew across the end, leaving the claws free. Wrap a length of yarn A several times around the bottom of each leg and arm. Fasten off. Attach

the body to the wings by sewing firmly along the central garter stitch line of the wings. Sew the legs onto the body using thread jointing (see Finishing Touches page 116). Sew arms onto shoulder of body, stretch them to the corner of each wing and secure the claws to this point with small stitches. Sew the tail onto the base of the body.

Facial features

Cut 2 teardrop-shaped pieces of white felt for eyes. Secure to sides of head with fabric glue. Sew two small green buttons on top. Using contrast thread, work three eyelashes at the outer edge of each eye using three straight stitches.

Finally, sew the head firmly onto the body of the Pterodactyl.

QUETZALCOATLUS

Named after the Aztec feather god, Quetzalcoatlus were the largest flying animals ever found with a wingspan of 36ft (11m) and a neck that stretched over 10ft (3m) long. Quetzalcoatlus probably hunted their prey by gliding toward the water and swooping up their meals. They filtered their food through long, toothless jaws.

Information you'll need

Finished size
Quetzalcoatlus measures 9¾in (25cm)

Materials
Stylecraft Life DK 75% acrylic, 25% wool (298m per 100g)
1 x 100g ball each in shades:
Daffodil (2394) (A)
Black (2307) (B)
Stylecraft Eskimo (5172) 100% polyester (90m per 50g)
1 x 50g ball in Ebony
1 pair of 3mm (UK11:US2–3) needles
Small piece of white felt for eyes
2 small green buttons (approx. ³⁄₁₆in/5mm)
Fabric glue
Polyester toy stuffing

Tension
26 sts and 36 rows to 4in (10cm) over st st using 3mm needles.
Use larger or smaller needles if necessary to obtain correct tension.

DID YOU KNOW?
Quetzalcoatlus had large brains and must have had good eyesight in order to spot prey from the air.

How to make Quetzalcoatlus

Wings
(make 1 in Ebony and 1 in A)
Cast on 3 sts.
Working in st st inc 1 st at each end of next and every foll row to 21 sts.
Work 1 row.
Inc 1 st the end of the next and every foll alt rows to 34 sts.
Work 15 rows.
Work 2 rows in g st.
Work 14 rows in st st.
Dec 1 st at the end of next and every foll alt rows to 21 sts.
Work 1 row.
Dec 1 st at each end of next and every foll row to 3 sts.
Next row: Sl1, k2tog, psso and fasten off.

Body and head:
worked from bottom to head
(make 1)
Using B, cast on 6 sts.
Work in st st and stripe pattern throughout until pattern states otherwise.

Stripe Patt: 2 rows B/2 rows A.
Row 1: Kfb into each st (12 sts).
Row 2 and every foll alt rows: Purl.
Row 3: (K1, kfb) 6 times (18 sts).
Row 5: (K2, kfb) 6 times (24 sts).
Row 7: (K3, kfb) 6 times (30 sts).
Work 19 rows.
Change to B and cont in this colour only:
Neck
Row 1: (K3, k2tog) 6 times (24 sts).
Row 2: Purl.
Row 3: (K2, k2tog) 6 times (18 sts).
Row 4: Purl.
Row 5: (K1, k2tog) 6 times (12 sts).
Row 6: Purl.
Row 7: K2tog, k8, k2tog (10sts).
Work 17 rows, inc 1 st at end of last row (11 sts).
Back of head
Row 1: Kfb, k3, kfb, k1, kfb, k3, kfb (15 sts).
Row 2: P7, k1, p7.
Row 3: Kfb, k5, kfb, k1, kfb, k5, kfb (19 sts).

Row 4: P9, k1, p9.
Row 5: Kfb, k7, kfb, k1, kfb, k7, kfb (23 sts).
Row 6: P11, k1, p11.
Row 7: Kfb, k9, kfb, k1, kfb, k9, kfb (27 sts).
Row 8: P13, k1, p13.
Row 9: Kfb, k10, ssk, k1, k2tog, k10, kfb (27 sts).
Row 10: As row 8.
Rep rows 9 and 10 once more.
Cast off.

Beak (make 1)
Using A, cast on 3 sts.
Working in st st inc 1 st at each end of next and every foll alt row to 17 sts.
Work 2 rows. Cast off.

Legs (make 2)
Using B, cast on 6 sts.
Work in st st until leg meas 6in (15cm), ending on a WS row.
Thigh
Change to Ebony and work 2 rows.
Row 1: Kfb into each st (12 sts).
Row 2 and every foll alt row: Purl.
Row 3: (K1, kfb) 6 times (18 sts).
Row 5: (K2, kfb) 6 times (24 sts).
Row 7: (K3, kfb) 6 times (30 sts).
Work 3 rows.
Row 11: (K3, k2tog) 6 times (24 sts).
Row 13: (K2, k2tog) 6 times (18 sts).
Row 15: (K1, k2tog) 6 times (12 sts).
Row 17: (K2tog) 6 times (6 sts).
Break yarn leaving a long tail, thread through rem sts and pull tight.

Arms (make 2)
Using B, cast on 6 sts.
Work in st st until arms meas 5in (13cm), ending on a WS row.
Cast off.

Making up

Darn in loose yarn ends.

Wings

With RS facing sew both parts of the wings together leaving a small hole for turning and stuffing. Turn RS out and stuff firmly. Close opening. Using contrast yarn, run a line of backstitch through all layers through the centre garter-stitch seam.

Body and head

Sew rear seam leaving a small hole for stuffing. Stuff firmly and close opening.

Beak

Fold in half lengthwise and sew rear seam. Stuff beak firmly, place over the front end of the head and stitch firmly in place.

Legs

Fold the furry thigh in half lengthwise and sew up leaving a small hole for stuffing. Stuff thigh firmly and close opening. Tie a knot in the end of the long string leg. Repeat for the second leg.

Arms

Tie a knot at one end of each arm. Now attach the body to the wings by sewing firmly along the central garter-stitch line of the wings. Sew the legs onto the body using thread jointing (see Finishing Touches page 116). Sew arms onto shoulder of body, stretch them out to the corner of each wing and secure the claws to this point with small stitches.

Facial features

Cut two teardrop-shaped pieces of white felt for eyes. Secure to sides of head with fabric glue. Sew two small green buttons on top. Take a long strand of Ebony Eskimo yarn and sew a few long loops to the top of Quetzalcoatlus' head. Secure at base and snip the loops to make a tuft.

How did dinosaurs manage without lemonade?

Can dinosaurs learn to knit?

Triceratops have how many horns?

When dinosaurs sleep, do they dino-snore?

Techniques

Getting started

Tools and materials

Getting started on your knitted dinosaur couldn't be easier. All you need are a few basic tools, DK or chunky-weight yarn, knitting needles, toy stuffing, felt and fabric glue – all of which are easily available from your local yarn or craft store.

Yarn substitution

If you are aiming for your dinosaur to look exactly as it appears on the pages of this book then you should use the yarn stated on the pattern. Information about where to source the specific yarns used can be found on page 121.

However, I have used DK or Chunky yarn throughout this book, which makes substituting extremely easy if that is what you prefer. Just scout your local yarn store for the same weight yarn i.e. DK or Chunky. As I mentioned in the introduction, although scientists know the shape and size of the dinosaurs, they had no idea what colour they were, so I heartily encourage using your own imagination when it comes to the finished character.

Tension

Designers are usually very specific about tension when it comes to the fit of a garment, and rightly so. However, in the case of your dinosaur, although I do state the tension in each pattern, it is not a disaster if your tension varies from this. What it will affect is the finished size of your dinosaur; for example, if it is looser, then your character will turn out bigger and likewise, if it is tighter, then he will be smaller. If you want him to turn out exactly like the one on the page, then check your tension first by knitting a tension swatch.

To knit a tension swatch, cast on 40 stitches using the recommended needle size. Work in pattern for 4in (10cm) minimum before casting off loosely. Next, lay the swatch out on a flat surface and place a flat ruler vertically on top. Count the number of rows over 4in (10cm). Then do the same horizontally but this time count the number of stitches over 4in (10cm). If you have more stitches and rows than stated on the pattern, try knitting the whole thing again using larger needles. If you have fewer stitches then repeat with smaller needles. Keep working at it until your tension matches that of the pattern.

Following instructions

Before you begin knitting, always read the pattern through from beginning to end. Then check any abbreviations you are not sure of against the list on page 122. Just like following a recipe, gather all your yarn, tools and notions together before you start.

Knitting techniques

Casting on

Thumb method

1 Make a slipknot a fair distance from the end of the yarn and place onto needle. Pull knot tight to make first stitch.

2 Hold needle in your right hand and wrap loose tail end around your left thumb from front to back. Push point of needle through the thumb loop from front to back. Wind the ball end of yarn around the needle from left to right.

3 Pull loop through thumb loop and remove thumb. Gently pull the new loop tight using the tail yarn. Repeat until you have desired amount of stitches on needle.

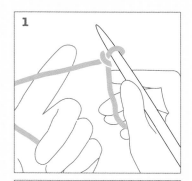

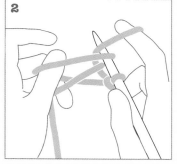

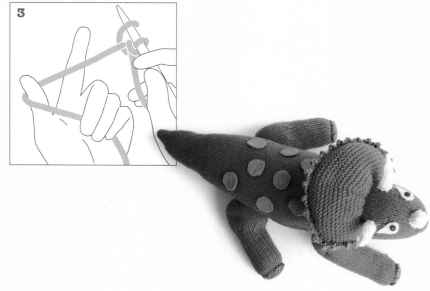

Knit stitch

1 Hold the needle with stitches in left hand. Hold yarn at back of work and insert point of right-hand empty needle into the front loop of the first stitch. Wrap yarn around point of right-hand needle in an anti-clockwise direction using your index finger. Bring yarn through to front of work.

2 With yarn still wrapped around the point, bring the right-hand needle back towards you through the loop of the first stitch. Try to keep the free yarn fairly taut but not too slack or tight.

3 Finally, with the new stitch firmly on the right-hand needle, gently pull the old stitch to the right and off the tip of the left-hand needle. Repeat for all the knit stitches across the row.

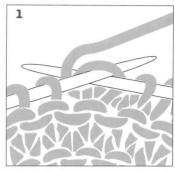

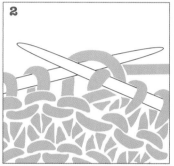

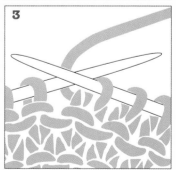

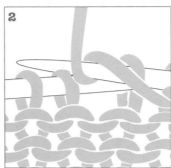
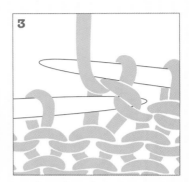

Purl stitch

1 Hold needles with stitches in left hand and hold yarn at front of work.

2 Insert point of right-hand empty needle into the front loop of the first stitch. Wrap yarn around point of right-hand needle in an anti-clockwise direction using index finger. Bring yarn back to front of work.

3 Now with yarn still wrapped around point of right-hand needle, bring it back through the stitch. Try to keep free yarn taut but not too slack or tight. Finally, with the new stitch firmly on the right-hand needle, gently pull the old stitch off the tip of the left-hand needle. Repeat for all the purl stitches along the row.

Other types of stitches

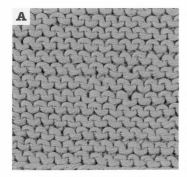

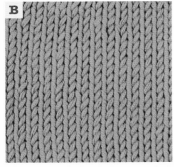

Garter stitch (A)
Knit every row.

Stocking stitch (B)
Knit on right-side rows and purl on wrong-side rows.

Casting off
1 Knit first two stitches. Push point of left needle through the first stitch and lift over the second stitch. One stitch remains on the right needle.

2 Knit another stitch from left needle and repeat step 1. Repeat until you have one stitch left. Cut yarn leaving a long tail and thread it through remaining stitch and pull tight.

Sewing up
For invisible seams always sew pieces together using matching yarn.

1 Place pieces to be joined side by side on a flat surface with right side facing towards you.

2 Take a threaded needle and secure to fabric by weaving down the side edge of one of the pieces. Bring the needle out between the first and second stitches.

3 Working vertically, bring the needle back up through the opposite piece and insert into first row again from front to back bringing it up below the horizontal strand.

4 Go back to first piece and keep stitching in this way. You will see your stitches form a ladder along the seam. Pull tight every few stitches to close fabric neatly.

Finishing touches

Stuffing your dinosaur

How you stuff your dinosaur will affect his final appearance and character. Always try to stuff firmly but beware of overstuffing, which stretches the knitting so the stuffing shows through on the outside.

I tend to stuff in small sections, filling the smaller spaces first such as heads and tails. Feed the stuffing through into tapered areas with the blunt end of a knitting needle and always mould and shape as you go. Keep holding him out and checking you are satisfied with the shape and silhouette before you go on. Finally, fill the larger areas like the tummy and legs, continuing to mould and shape to the very end. Make a final check on the shape before you close the stuffing hole.

Thread jointing your dinosaur

It is fun to make your dinosaur walk and be able to move his arms and legs around. I have used a technique called thread jointing on some of the more upright characters so they can walk and fight each other freely. This technique is very simple and works as follows:

1 Pin the arms or legs to the sides of the body.

2 Thread a needle with a long piece of thread and double it for strength.

3 Push the needle through one side of the body at the pin position, take it through the limb, and then right through the body to the opposite side then finally, through the opposite limb.

4 Now go back through the body in the opposite direction, taking the needle through all layers and coming out on the opposite side through that limb.

5 Repeat this process until the limbs are secure, pulling the thread tightly each time so you get a little dimple where the needle enters and exits the limb.

6 When you are satisfied you have secured the limb properly, fasten off.

Attaching the eyes

I have used small buttons and felt pieces stuck on with fabric glue for the eyes throughout this book. I recommend using a good-quality glue that is not PVA based. This is because PVA glue doesn't stand up to washing in hot water and if your dinosaur is to be well loved and washed, then this could be a problem.

Safety warning

If you are giving dinosaurs to very small children or babies then I recommend that you do not use buttons for eyes. French knots sewn in a contrast colour (see page 118) can be used instead. The felt pieces can also be sewn in place with backstitch, which is more secure.

Steggie is the best out of all his friends in a staring match.

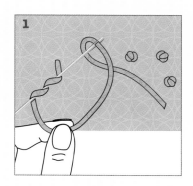 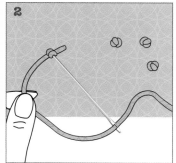

French knots

Work in any direction.

1 Bring needle to RS of fabric. Holding thread taut with finger and thumb of left hand, wind thread once or twice around needle tip.

2 Still holding thread, insert needle tip close to the point where you brought the needle out to the RS of fabric and pull needle to back of work so the twist lies neatly on the fabric surface. Repeat as required.

This knitting lark is very tiring.

Do museums have old dinosaur bones because they can't afford new ones?

Back stitch

Work from right to left. Bring needle up to right side of work at point 1, down at point 2 and back up at 3. Try to keep the distance between stitches even. Begin next stitch at point 1. Repeat as required.

Caring for your dinosaur

Hopefully, your dinosaur characters will be loved
and appreciated. However, in the event that they
become a bit too well loved, you can wash them if you
stick to the following rules. Hand wash only in warm
water with a small amount of regular soap powder.
Do not agitate or rub too hard. Squeeze out excess water
gently. Do not wring or rub. Coax the dinosaur back
into shape and leave to dry naturally.

Yarn suppliers

Artesano from Yarn Box
E-mail: info@yarnbox.co.uk
Tel: +44 (0)7791 639896

King Cole Ltd
Snaygill Industrial Estate
Keighley Road
Skipton
North Yorkshire
BD23 2QR
United Kingdom
Tel: +44 (0)1756 703670

Rico Yarn
Rico Design
Industriestrasse 19–23
D–33034 Brakel
Germany
www.rico-design.co.uk

Sirdar Spinning Ltd
Flanshaw Lane
Wakefield
West Yorkshire
WF2 9ND
United Kingdom
Tel: +44 (0)1924 371501
www.sirdar.co.uk

Stylecraft
Spectrum Yarns
Spa Mill
Slaithwaite
Huddersfield
West Yorkshire
HD7 5BB
United Kingdom
Tel: +44 (0)1484 848435
www.stylecraft-yarns.co.uk

Abbreviations

alt	alternate
approx	approximately
beg	beginning
CC	contrast colour
cm	centimetres
CO	cast on
cont	continue
dec	decrease
DK	double knit
foll	following
g st	garter stitch
inc	increase by working into front and back of same stitch
in	inches
K	knit
kfb	increase by working into front and back of same stitch
k2tog	decrease by knitting 2 stitches together
kwise	by knitting the st
meas	measures
MB	(k1,yf,k1,yf,k1) into next st, turn, p5, turn, k5, turn, p2tog, p1, p2tog, turn, sl1, k2tog, psso
MC	main colour
P	purl

patt	pattern
p2tog	purl 2 together
p2togtbl	purl 2 together through the back loops
pfb	purl into front and back of next st
psso	pass slipped stitch over
PUK	pick up and knit
rem	remaining
rep	repeat
RH	right hand
RS	right side
sl	slip
sl st	slip stitch
ssk	slip the next 2 stitches knitwise, slip back on LH needle and knit 2 together
st(s)	stitch(es)
st st	stocking stitch
tog	together
tbl	through back of the loop
WS	wrong side
yf	yarn over
*****	work instructions immediately following *, then rep as directed.
( )	rep instructions inside brackets as many times as instructed

I wish I could knit, but my flippers keep getting in the way.

Conversions

Knitting needles

UK:	Metric:	US:
14	*2mm*	0
13	*2.25mm*	1
12	*2.75mm*	2
11	*3mm*	–
10	*3.25mm*	3
–	*3.5mm*	4
9	*3.75mm*	5
8	*4mm*	6
7	*4.5mm*	7
6	*5mm*	8
5	*5.5mm*	9
4	*6mm*	10
3	*6.5mm*	10.5
2	*7mm*	10.5
1	*7.5mm*	11
0	*8mm*	13
000	*10mm*	15

Yarn weight

UK:	US:
2-ply	Lace
3-ply	Fingering
4-ply	Sport
Double knitting	Light worsted
Aran	Fisherman/worsted
Chunky	Bulky
Super chunky	Extra bulky

Terms

UK:	US:
Cast off	Bind off
Tension	Gauge

Dinosaur names

Dinosaur names can be tricky to pronounce. Here is a phonetic guide so you can practise saying them. Dinosaurs are usually named by the person who discovered them. They are often Greek or Latin words and can describe something about the dinosaur's behaviour, size, shape, the location they were first found or sometimes after a person or mythological figure.

Diplodocus
dih-plod-uh-kus
meaning: double beam

Triceratops:
try-sair-uh-tops
meaning: three-horned face

Ankylosaurus:
ang-kile-uh-sawr-us
meaning: fused lizard

Stegosaurus
steg-uh-sawr-us
meaning: roof lizard

Parasaurolophus
par-ah-sawr-ol-uh-fus
meaning: crested lizard

Tyrannosaurus Rex
tye-ran-uh-sawr-us
meaning: tyrant king

Allosaurus
al-uh-sawr-us
meaning: other lizard

Velociraptor
veh-loss-ih-rap-tor
meaning: fast robber

Troodon
tro-uh-don
meaning: gnaw tooth

Spinosaurus
spy-nuh-sawr-us
meaning: thorn lizard

Plesiosaur
plee-see-uh-sohr
meaning: close to lizard

Ichthyosaurus
ikh-thee-oh-sawr-us
meaning: fish lizard

Mesosaurus
Mezz-owe-sawr-us
meaning: middle lizard

 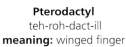

Pterodactyl
teh-roh-dact-ill
meaning: winged finger

Quetzalcoatlus
kwet-zal-coat-lus
meaning: named after
the Aztec's god, Quetzalcoatl

125

About the author

Tina Barrett was taught to knit by her grandmother and has been passionate about creating her own gorgeous yarn and fabric-based designs ever since. She is a regular contributor to many knitting and sewing magazines and is the author of several books for GMC Publications, including *Home Sewn Nursery*, *Knits for Dogs & Cats*, *Natural Knits for Babies & Toddlers*, *Fat Quarter: One-Piece Projects* and *Natural Crochet for Babies & Toddlers*. Tina lives with her family in Cornwall in the south-west of England.

Author acknowledgements

Thanks must go to Gerrie Purcell at GMC for approaching me with the idea for this fun Jurassic book in the first place. Also, thanks to Virginia Brehaut for excellent editorial skills, Sarah Hatton for her pattern checking and to all the guys who made such a wonderful job of the books styling and artwork. A huge, big thanks to Rebecca Mothersole who took such fabulous photographs.

Special thanks goes to all those who shared enthusiasm for the project and donated yarn and notions. I hope I have done you all proud: Tom and Jenny Comber of Artesano, David Rawson at Rico Yarns, Jane Jubb at Sirdar Yarns, Jill Penny-Larter at Stylecraft Yarns and Lance Martin at King Cole.

Finally, a big hug to all my family for loving these woolly dinosaurs as much as I do. Those scary dudes (the dinosaurs, not my family!) developed as characters in their own right as soon as they appeared from my needles. When I sent them off to be photographed and styled, I confess that I felt a twinge of sadness. Like I was sending my children off into the big bad world for the first time, which shows how much fun I had making them all or, conversely, that I really do need to get out more!

Index

To place an order, or to request a catalogue, contact:
GMC Publications Ltd
Castle Place, 166 High Street, Lewes, East Sussex, BN7 1XU
United Kingdom
Tel: +44 (0)1273 488005
www.gmcbooks.com